Rent It Up!

Four Steps to Unlocking the Profit
Potential in Your Self-Storage Business

TRON JORDHEIM

Rent It Up!: Four Steps to Unlocking the Profit Potential in Your Self-Storage Business

Published by Wheatmark®
610 East Delano Street, Suite 104
Tucson, Arizona 85705 U.S.A.
www.wheatmark.com

International Standard Book Number: 978-1-60494-208-8
Library of Congress Control Number: 2008938874

Contents

Introduction

The self-storage business can be a profitable business. A well-built, well-presented facility in a good location should do well enough. However, the difference between doing well enough and doing very well can be quite significant. How do you get beyond just doing well and start doing very well? You do that by focusing on sales and marketing.

Self-storage used to be a property management game. It still is, but sales and marketing are becoming very important elements. There is an extra 10 to 15 percent boost in revenue that can be gained by focusing on sales and marketing. Real economic upside comes from the strategies and tactics I will outline for you in this book. Here are the four ways to push profits in your self-storage business:

1. Create a selling culture
2. Learn the basics of sales
3. Apply sales skills to self-storage
4. Get inside your customer's mind

Creating a Selling Culture

Why do we want to create a selling culture? What's the point? It's a lot of work. It's a lot of trouble. It is going to throw your current operations into a certain amount of chaos.

Creating a selling culture will require good leadership and good management skills from you and your staff. Some of your favorite employees are going to have a hard time adjusting. You're going to end up firing a few people you like because they won't fit in the new system. You're going to have a hard time finding people to hire as new employees who have what it takes to thrive in a sales culture. Not all of the people you think will work out actually will end up working out for you. You are going to devote time, money, and effort. So what's the point?

Would you agree that it's better to have a sales-savvy staff than to not have a sales-savvy staff? Okay, great! That is the jumping-off point. Call it strategy; call it philosophy; call it keeping up with your competition. If you believe you should have a sales culture, then the work of creating a sales culture will be worth the reward.

There is a school of thought that says, "Don't worry about sales. If you have a decent location, and your rates are okay, and you do a lot of advertising, then it doesn't matter. As long as people come in, you can rent to enough of them, and you don't have to have very good salespeople at the store." Do you subscribe to that theory? If you do, you may be looking at the wrong book. You should be looking at *Good Enough: Five Easy Ways to Make a Little Profit in Self-Storage without Putting out Much Effort, Time, or Money.*

Perhaps the "good enough" strategy is not such a bad strategy. It's a lot less trouble and a lot less expensive. You will invest a lot less sweat and energy. If you are happy getting a little cash flow without running a very good business or without building much value into your real estate asset, then go for it. Be just "good enough."

But if you are trying to create as much profit as you can and build a sustainable business, as well as a real estate asset that will increase in value far faster than your competitors', then you are in the right place, and you should keep on reading.

What is the operational result of creating the selling culture? There are three results in store for you: renting to more people, keeping current renters longer, and generating more revenue per customer. If you could rent to two or three more people a month than you do now, what is the actual added value to you? What do you think a rental at your property is worth, maybe six hundred dollars by the time the customer has moved in, bought insurance and boxes, and moved out again? Maybe at your property, the value's closer to a thousand dollars or more? No matter what sort of a market you are in, there's a lot of money involved, isn't there?

Now let me also ask you this: Are you getting a significant amount of your new business from referrals? Do you think you're getting up to 20 percent of your new business from referrals? Are you getting more than 20 percent? Let's go with 20 percent for the sake of this example. If that is the case, the added value of the new customer has even more impact than just the revenue he or she creates alone. If you get five new renters, you will receive one additional renter from a referral. So you are buying six customers for the price of five. That is one heck of a deal, don't you think?

In businesses that are not focused on a sales culture, the number of referrals might be significantly lower. They may be buying eleven customers for the price of ten or twenty-one customers for the price of twenty. That doesn't sound nearly as good, does it? This is just one reason why creating a selling culture is so important.

Another part of the puzzle is keeping tenants longer. It doesn't do you any good if you rent to more people but even more people move out, correct? So what would the added value be to you if your customer stayed an extra month or two or three? It would be tremendous, right? If your average customer is staying eight months and generates eight hundred dollars in rental income, wouldn't an average length of stay of ten months generate ten thousand dollars in revenue?

An increase of two months in length of stay could easily increase the average revenue per customer by 20 percent. Wouldn't you feel good about a 20 percent increase in revenue? An increase in length of stay would also have a tremendous impact on occupancy rates and time-on-market ratios of empty units. What would happen to the asset value of your business if your occupancy rates jumped 10 percent?

In many cases, this increase would cause your property to be considered "stabilized" or "highly occupied." Lenders love that! You could refinance your property under much more favorable terms, which would allow you to send even more dollars to the bottom line.

If your selling culture is working, you're also cross-selling and up-selling with better proficiency, moving more products and supplies out the door. This might mean that your thousand-dollar customer is now an eleven-hundred-dollar customer. It just keeps getting better.

The ultimate result of your selling culture is a significant rise in your asset's value. If the value of your business is its revenue times your cap rate, it is not unusual for your company's value to be ten or twelve times its revenue. If this is true, then every dollar you create translates into ten or twelve dollars in value. This ought to be enough motivation to make you a selling culture maniac.

It sounds easy enough, doesn't it? Well, on the one hand, it is very simple. The whole storage experience can be boiled down to pain-and-pleasure stimulus. The behavior of customers continues to be strongly influenced by basic instinct: avoid pain and seek pleasure.

Is it a pain for customers to move into your place, or do you make it easy for them? Is it a pleasure to stay there? Is it a pain to move out? Or do people move out because it's a pain to stay? Managing the pains and pleasures people associate with your business lays the foundation for creating your sales culture.

I got my start in the selling culture in the sixth grade. Many of my friends had jobs. Most of the kids my age were sacking or delivering groceries, and I thought those guys worked awfully hard for next to no money. I noticed there were glass windows everywhere along the retail streets where I lived in Brooklyn, New York. There were only adults washing windows with buckets, squeegees, and ladders. But I could reach most of the glass without a ladder, and I could buy window cleaner in a spray can.

So I got myself a roll of towels and a can of window cleaner and started a window cleaning business. I stopped in on all the small retail businesses and offices that lined the main shopping street in my neighborhood and created a little office window cleaning route for myself. The small business owners thought it was cute to let an ambitious kid have their business, especially since I was a lot cheaper than an established cleaning business. I was making three times what my buddies were making delivering groceries, and I thought, *You know, this entrepreneur life isn't bad.* And I've been at it ever since. I've started companies from nothing and turned them into something. I've managed salespeople, run marketing programs, created business models, and sent lots of dollars to the bottom line.

I learned about self-storage selling cultures by helping to create The PhoneSmart Off-Site Sales Force. Storage Mart founded PhoneSmart to serve as a call center that would turn missed phone calls at self-storage properties into rental opportunities. Storage Mart created PhoneSmart not just to grow its own business, but to serve other storage owners who were looking for ways to improve their businesses. We created selling systems, training systems, sales auditing systems, and new ways to generate customers. This has helped us to learn how self-storage customers think and act and how owners and managers of self-storage properties think and act. In our first six years of doing business, we served storage properties in forty-seven states and five Canadian provinces and had more than a million conversations with self-storage customers and prospective customers. We sent our clients more than three hundred twenty-five thousand leads and reservations. We continue to tweak our systems and create new service offerings that help our clients rent to more people, keep them longer, and generate more revenue from each customer. Our business thrives by constantly raising the bar in the industry.

My point is that we have real-world, successful, day-to-day knowledge to pass on to you. My PhoneSmart commercial is over. If you want to find out more about us and how we do what we do, go to selfstorageblog.com or phone-smart.info.

Let's concentrate on getting a selling culture working in your business. How do you build a selling culture? How do you build any culture? I go to trade shows and conferences in Las Vegas fairly often. I think Las Vegas is a fascinating place to see because it has such a powerful gaming culture, at least on The Strip. When you consider the history of Las Vegas, the gaming culture is what created the place and allowed it to diversify into a regional center of commerce, tourism, and development. Once you get off The Strip, you realize that many of the people who live in Las Vegas could care less what happens on The Strip; but everyone in this town lives to some degree off of the ripples of the gaming culture. So a culture can be powerful.

How do you create a selling culture, then? What makes any kind of culture? If you ever took an interest in anthropology or sociology, then you know that stories, myths, language, ritual, and clothing are the things that create a culture. We have some clients in Canada, and a lot of folks think that all you have to do to be a Canadian is just to use a long "o" when you say the word "process" and make the word "about" sound like "a boot." That's it. Two simple words and you are in the Canadian club. Many Canadians will actually think you are Canadian, too, if you use these two words. This actually works, by the way. When we are making secret shopping phone calls to Canadian clients, we can pass for compatriots by talking with a neutral North American accent and adding the Canadian pronunciation of "process" and "about."

The hip-hop culture continues to thrive all over the world. You see young people who appear to be into the hip-hop culture, and it seems that all you have to do to be able to get into the hip-hop culture is just say "yo" every once in a while and wear baggy, low-riding pants.

Sometimes what makes someone think you're a member of one culture or another can be something very simple. I like to wear construction boots and jeans when the weather gets a little wet and rainy. If it is cold and wet outside, I'll wear my Carhartt jacket and my favorite yellow baseball cap that has a Caterpillar logo on it. I have been taken for a construction worker many times. Now I suppose I am in the construction business, from a certain point of view. I construct businesses and sales and marketing processes, and I construct books. But I am not sure I could last a full day on a house-framing crew without taking a nap from 2:00 to 4:00 PM.

People are quick to categorize you by the way they see you. You may not like that people don't see you for who you are but for what they think you are. You may not like to be pigeonholed for the way you might appear or sound. But you can make this work to your benefit. Why do so many professions have a uniform? Because it tells the world clearly who is a firefighter or nurse, so the firefighter or nurse can do his or her job quickly and efficiently.

I did a simple test when I ran a Culligan Bottled Water dealership. I believed that the route drivers were invisible to people and could go where they wanted, when they wanted, without restrictions. One day, I went cold-calling for new customers in a business area, wearing the water delivery driver's uniform. The very next day, I called on the same businesses in a suit and tie. No one recognized me as being the same person. Only a few said that another guy had been through the day before, but no one knew it was me.

I tested my theory further. I walked into a bank that was not our customer with a five-gallon bottle on my shoulder and strolled back behind the teller's counter and back into the break room where I was not supposed to be. No one stopped me. No one asked who I was or where I was going. I had to ask someone in the break room who I would talk to about setting them up with water service before anyone even acknowledged me.

They thought I was a member of the service culture and that I was doing something I was supposed to be doing. I was invisible. So we used this to our advantage and dressed all of our salespeople in route driver uniforms and built one of the top bottled water dealerships in the entire Culligan dealership network. Our sales people appeared invisible at first and then non-threatening when noticed. This allowed them access to decision makers and the ability to set many, many free trials, which created a swift growth of customers.

How do you want your people pigeonholed? Don't you want your customers thinking your people are members of the selling culture? Because don't people love a good sales experience? If you go to a store, and you're looking to buy something, doesn't it drive you crazy if the people ignore you and don't help you or don't help you figure out what to buy? This drives me crazy. Let's not do that to our customers. Let's make sure our prospective customers and our current customers see us as members of a selling culture who are there to help them make their purchases.

What are some of the stories and myths and some of the language we can use to build a selling culture? Well, let's talk the language of sales. If you talk about suspects and prospects and clients and closing ratios and things of that nature, your staff starts thinking like salespeople. If you start talking like salespeople, you start thinking like salespeople.

I don't know if any of these terms are foreign to you or not, but I'll run through a few phrases really quickly. This may just be a review, but that's okay.

A "suspect" is someone you hope might, could, or should do business with you. People in the storage business don't talk to very many suspects, unless you go out and knock on doors in the neighborhood around your storage facility.

The people who call you on the phone and the people who walk into your place are "prospects" because they've identified that they either have a need for what you sell or think a need is coming up. Prospects have expressed some need or desire for what you have to offer.

"Closing ratios" or "conversion ratios" tell you how many prospects you are required to get a customer: the ratio of prospects to customers. These ratios can change dramatically based on where your prospects come from. In self-storage, you typically get prospects from people who see your location from traveling by it, people who find your ad in the yellow pages, Internet users who see your website, Internet users who submit their information to storage locator services, referrals from current customers, repeat customers, mailers, fliers, and other marketing efforts. You should know your business's ratios on all of these so you can better manage your advertising, marketing and sales efforts, and better judge when you are doing something right or when you are missing the mark.

Learn the vocabulary of selling and then talk about the process of selling. Talk about "qualifying questions," things like, "Do you know how soon you're going to need a storage unit?" "Do you have an idea of what size you need, or can I help you figure that out?" "Do you know where we're located, and is that a good location for you?" Design and frame your qualifiers intentionally.

Are you familiar with "closing questions"? Is that a term you use in your property? If you use the term, do you actually ask closing questions to your prospects?

"When would you like to move in?" "Is Saturday a good time for you to come in, or is Sunday better?" "Would you like the ten-foot-by-ten-foot or would you prefer the ten-foot-by-fifteen-foot?" If your people understand what closing questions are, they'll use them, and your culture will develop.

I have heard some people call a closing question "the ask." This is not a bad concept. When you get to the right point in your conversation with your prospect and you have asked good qualifying questions, it is time for "the ask." You ask the prospect to make the purchase.

I have heard others say that using the term "close" sounds a little crude and adversarial, as if your prospect might get hurt when you "close" them. This is not a bad point either. Maybe we are really asking people to "open" an account with us or to "open" a business relationship with us. I like this way of thinking. It shines a positive light on the way in which you ask someone to be your customer.

Do you see what is happening here? By talking about sales issues in the language of selling, we are participating in the culture of sales. Help your people be in the culture of sales by talking about selling.

Talk about some cost issues. A selling culture knows what it takes to make money. What does it actually cost you to get a rental inquiry? Do you know what a telephone call costs your property? Have you done the math? I think you would be shocked to see how much it costs to actually make the phone ring. Now take that one step further and try to figure out what each telephone rental inquiry costs you. Take your marketing and advertising budget and figure out how many phone call rental inquiries you generate. Go even another step and figure out where these telephone inquiries came from. People are getting your phone number from many different sources. If you knew all those sources and the power of each of them, it would shake you up! Despite the cost and importance of telephone inquiries, many properties count only 8 to 10 percent of phone calls as rental inquiries. Isn't that a little scary? Doesn't this make each phone call even that much more important?

I know you'd like to think that half of your phone calls are new rental inquiries. Is that fantasy or reality? Find out!

What does it actually cost you for an acquisition? Can you segment out each of your sources and get a close estimate on what each class of rental costs? You may find some of your most expensive types of customers to acquire are your shortest stays. Maybe they are your longest stays? How can you drive that cost lower? How do you find more of the customers that are less expensive? How can you capture some of the rental opportunities that you're not catching? Talking about the costs associated with opening new accounts makes your staff think like salespeople.

One of the sales topics I like to talk about is the idea of "concerns and assurances." Are you familiar with the terms "objections" and "rebuttals"? These are ways of talking about the reasons people do not buy and the things we can do or say to overcome a reason for not buying.

Do you like the terms "objection" and "rebuttal"? Objection and rebuttal sound like something that happens in a courtroom when there is a bitter dispute over facts. It sounds rude and adversarial to give a rebuttal to your prospect. I realize you often have to fight to win a customer, but I don't think you should be fighting *with* the potential customer. Making a decision to buy is not an act of submission to the salesperson. I don't think our prospects come in and say, "I object to the size of that unit you are offering me. I will not take that size!" What they do is say to themselves, *Well, I'm not sure about this. I'm not sure about that. I'm not sure about something else.* They have concerns about making a good decision.

So if your salespeople are great at assuring your potential clients that they are making a good choice when they rent with you, then you've made the sale, and you've made great strides in creating your selling culture.

Your selling culture succeeds when its main focus is helping people find that it is comfortable to decide to buy from you.

I'll give you a little million-dollar tip. There's a wonderful method of assuring customers that your offering is a good choice. It is called the "feel-felt-found." And you're all using this method now at your store to a certain extent, whether you know it or not. There are other ancient and reliable sales methods you are using at your store that already have names and have been handed down from one generation of salespeople to the next, just like the stories and traditions of other cultures. Only you don't know their names; nor do you know how to use them correctly. I am here to help you get back in touch with the roots of the culture of selling. I'll help you by telling you about "feel-felt-found."

"Feel-felt-found" goes like this: "I understand how you feel about paying that much rent for a storage unit. Some of our other customers felt that way too before they moved in to their units. But what they found was our place is a great place to store. That's why a large portion of our business comes from repeat customers and referrals."

That's how the "feel-felt-found" works, and it works with every concern that people have when they talk to you. "I understand how you feel about the price of our ten by ten. Some people felt like it was a lot of money too, but what they found was that, with the features and amenities that we offer at this store, it was a great storage experience. So I can assure you you're going to like renting here. Would you like to move in today, or would tomorrow be better for you?" It's a powerful technique. You can customize it to your own way of speaking, and you can use it all day long and never get tired of it.

Do not look at the things preventing a prospect from saying, "Sure, I'll rent from you now" as objections. They are only concerns. Treat them as concerns.

Another sales issue that is important to talk about is the concept and practice of follow-up. We'd like to think that prospects make up their mind quickly and decide to rent within a few days of deciding they might need to store some things. The fact is that there are many different timeframes for different classes of storage prospects. You can rent to at least 30 percent of the people you talk to today in the future, even when they can not make a decision today. Even if you did everything in your power to help them decide today, they can't all decide today.

You are letting your competitors rent to lots of your prospects because you are letting prospects get away from you. Do you think you are doing follow-up very well? Come up with a great follow-up system to make sure that everyone you talk to either rents from you now or rents from you later—because your prospects are not shoppers; they're buyers, aren't they? They don't stop at your property because they think the flowerbed out in front is pretty and they want to come check it out. They stop because they have an immediate need or their spouses told them they're going to have an immediate need. People do not browse in a storage facility. They do not tour your property to kill a little time. They do not bring their kids to your site just to let the kids blow off a little steam. They are buyers. So they're either going to buy from you, or you are going to let them buy from someone else. In a few cases their situation is going to change and they're not going to buy from anyone. So get a follow-up system in place. It is what a selling culture would do.

What are some of the goals and targets that you need to promote with your staff? Some of them, such as occupancy goals, are fairly obvious. But do your staff people know that you're looking at both physical occupancy and economic occupancy? Do they know the difference? Do they know that it's okay sometimes if your physical occupancy is falling off, as long as your economic occupancy is growing? What about revenue goals? Do your staff people understand that, when it's time for price increases, it's okay to lose a few renters? You have work to do building your sales culture so they understand the goals and targets you're shooting at.

Do you have great systems for cross-selling, up-selling, and re-selling? Does anyone even talk about these topics at your stores? Many times when I am traveling, I will have a coffee and a muffin for a quick breakfast. I love watching the pros at the well-established coffee shops move people through the line. They're fantastic. They move you through that line fast. That part is wonderful. But what they don't do is they don't up-sell. When they ask you, "Yes, can I help you? What would you like?" and you say, "I'd like a coffee and a muffin," they don't say, "Well, have you tried the Danish?" or "Would you like a second muffin to take with you for later?"

If they did ask, and every third person took them up on the offer of the Danish or second muffin, they could be looking at a 15- to 20-percent boost in revenue. Wouldn't that be something?

But they've got the operations down pat; they've got the system of moving people through the shop quickly well in hand. So is that what you have at your store? Do you have a great way to move people in quickly and efficiently but forget to sell boxes and locks and renter's insurance?

What are some of the revenue targets you have, and do your people know what your revenue targets are? If you're in a lease-up situation, does your staff know how many units you've promised your lenders and partners you're going to rent this month? If they don't, you need to plug them into that information. Get them on the team. I assure you, the entire offensive line of a football team knows what they have to do during a game: They have to give the quarterback enough time to get his aim right. They have to block right on some plays, block left on others, and let the defensive players through the line on yet other plays. They know their roles in every play in the book. Do your staff people even know there is a playbook for self-storage? How can you build stories and myths about the great plays that have been made by your people if they don't even know there is a playbook?

Let's talk about some of the myths and stories that build a culture. Do you know any little kids that have seen many of the Disney movies? Okay. These movies lay the foundation of our American popular culture. A little kid who hasn't seen *High School Musical*, *Cinderella*, or *Finding Nemo*, or at least *The Lion King* is not in our culture. He or she might as well live on the moon!

If Disney tells the stories that help build our pop culture, what kind of myths and stories help build a selling culture? Let's think about that for a minute. One of the stories I love is called the "Rule of Thirds." There's actually a "Rule of Thirds" for many different kinds of situations because it's easy to remember three things, and it's easy to draw a triangle. Here's how our "Rule of Thirds" goes: One group of people is going to rent from you anyway, no matter what, as long as you don't say something stupid or chase them off because they've already decided they like your place. They know someone who's rented there. Maybe they drive by it every day and think it looks good. Whatever the reason is, they've already decided they're going to rent from you, and when they come to see you or call you on the phone, what they're really trying to find out is if they shouldn't rent from you. In their minds, they are asking themselves if their inclination to rent from you is wrong. So when you get someone in this easy third, your job is to not drive them off and to just let them rent the unit.

You have another group of people who aren't going to rent from you anyway, no matter what you do because their situation is going to change: the house doesn't sell; the divorce doesn't come through. The situation changes. Their Uncle Fred says, "Don't pay for storage. I've got a barn you can use for free." Something will happen to those people; you'll lose them without any wrongdoing of your own. Your job with those people is to give them as good an experience as you can so when it is time for them to actually need to store, they'll think of you and contact you first so you can rent to them at some future date.

But then there is this third group of people who could go either way. They're not quite sure what they're doing. They're not quite sure they're going to store. They're not quite sure they're going to store with you. They're not quite sure they like your place. They're not quite sure they can afford your place. This group of people who can go either way are the people who help you make your money because they represent the "upside" in your promotional spending.

Anyone who is halfway friendly can rent to that easy third, but only people with sales skills and persistence and people who see themselves in a selling culture can work with that third that can go either way. If you can convert a nice share of that either-way third, those dollars go right to your bottom line. These people that you might not have rented to before you adopted a selling culture are the people who represent your increase in revenue. So keep the Rule of Thirds in mind when you're talking to prospects. Is this person in the easy third? If so, just move him in. Is this person in the impossible third? I'll give you an example of a person in the impossible third.

We actually got this phone call at our PhoneSmart call center. One of our supervisors, Dana Shields, was catching calls for our many self-storage clients. She asked the fellow who called, "How soon are you going to need a storage unit?" and he said, "Well, I'm retiring in four years. I won't need it until then, but I'm just curious what one costs." So there's a prepared man! He's certainly in the impossible third because, no matter how great you are at sales and service, he is not going to retire this week just to start renting a storage unit from you.

But then you talk to all of the other people who say, "Well, I still have to shop around"; "That's maybe a little more than I'm looking to spend"; "I'm not sure if I'm ready to do anything yet"; "I've got to check with my boss"; "I've got to check with my spouse." When you can rent to a large portion of these people, that's when you make your money.

Here is another fun rule of selling. It's called the "Chuckle Rule," and it goes like this: for every chuckle you get from your prospects, the odds of you doing business with them double. If you get two chuckles, the odds are four times as good. Now there's a point of diminishing returns in there somewhere around the third to fifth chuckle, when the people are laughing so hard that they leave your store, or they have had enough and would like to get down to business. But keep the "chuckle rule" in mind. It's a very, very important rule because that moment of laughter gives you great rapport with people. Having that rapport allows you to really talk openly and honestly with prospective customers. It means they are likely to follow your recommendations. It means you can be a little assertive in dealing with them.

I was talking to one of our clients recently who was telling me about how the "chuckle rule" had helped him make a rental. Someone had walked into the store, and they'd shared a few laughs. The potential customer told our client he was not ready to rent anything yet and started to walk out the door. Our client, the store manager, said, "Oh, come on now, you know you're going to need it Saturday. Isn't the best thing to just get it today and start getting organized before Saturday?" And the guy turned around and said, "Yeah, you're probably right. Okay." Not the most sophisticated close in the world, but it worked because he had shared a few chuckles and had established some rapport. He didn't have to be particularly smooth when he tried one more time to get the rental. He just had to try. The "chuckle rule" is a powerful technique.

Stories are a great way to foster a culture. There are some great stories that can help your staff relate to selling. Have you ever gone ice fishing? I lived in Wisconsin as a kid, and not only did we do some ice fishing, but it was lots of fun to take cars out and drive around on the frozen lakes. If you are not accustomed to the ice culture, you might say, "What, are you guys nuts?" I'd say, "Well, yes, but the ice was thick!" There are, of course, always stories about the people who went out on the ice a day too early in the season or a day too late. There are more than a few cars and snowmobiles at the bottom of Wisconsin lakes.

Greg Tyler told me this story, and you should tell it to your staff. Greg is a storyteller from Columbia, Missouri, and he has many wonderful stories to share. This story is part of the oral tradition of the selling culture. You have to pass on the good stories.

Anyway, here's how the story goes: If you know a little bit about ice fishing, you know it is its own culture, and you can buy as much gear for ice fishing as you can for anything else. There was this one guy who bought all of the gear. He had the fancy icehouse that he could pull out on a trailer, with his TV and VCR, a heater and satellite connection, and everything else you'd want in there. He had his automatic fish finder, his power auger to get through the ice, and the most expensive ice fishing pole one could buy. He was sitting there one day with his hook down in the water. Nothing happened. Not a single nibble.

He looked out the double-paned, insulated glass of his fishing hut and saw a little kid walk up to a spot in the ice not too far from him with a bucket in his hand and a hatchet. The kid turned the bucket upside down, sat down on the bucket, took the hatchet and chopped a little hole in the ice, and threw a string with a hook down in the hole. The guy in the fancy ice hut watched for a little while because he thought this was pretty funny. He started ice fishing the same way when he was a kid. He laughed, thinking of how frustrated the kid would be sitting out in the freezing cold on his bucket all day trying to catch one fish.

Our friend in the fancy icehouse was eager to start piling up all the fish his expensive gear would help him catch and was about to go back to his ice hole when the kid pulled out a fish. The guy chuckled. He thought, "Isn't that cute? Beginner's luck." The guy felt a little annoyed because he had already been out there for a while, and he had nothing to show for it.

He was about to sit back down at his ice hole when he flipped to the golf channel on his satellite TV. Just then, out of the corner of his eye, he saw the kid pull another fish out of the lake. And then the kid pulled another one out.

Now our well-geared friend was starting to get a little annoyed because his six-thousand-dollar fish finder wasn't helping him at all. So he got out of his seventy-two-degree ice house and walked over to the kid and said, "Hey, kid, what's your secret?"

And the kid says, "Mum ah mum mum," or something like that.

The guy, having no idea what the kid said, thought, *Oh, great! The kid is Special Ed, too!*

He turned around and went back in his icehouse. He threw his hook in again; nothing happened. Not a nibble. He sat there for a few minutes that seemed like an hour. He looked out the window again, and the kid's got three more fish up on the ice. Now he's really starting to get mad.

So he got out, walked over to the kid, and said, "Kid, I've got to know your secret."

The kid said, "Mum ah mum mum."

And the guy said, "Look, kid, I can't understand your gibberish. You've got to tell me; what's your secret?"

So the kid held his hand up in front of his mouth, spat some worms out into his hand, and said, quite matter-of-factly, "Keep your bait warm!"

You can imagine that our friend with all the fancy gear stood humbled for at least a moment or two.

What do you do to keep the bait warm in your business? Do you have a warm, friendly smile when people come in? Are you sure to make an extra walk around the property to see that there's no litter floating around your place? Is the unit that you're showing your customer actually swept out? Are you keeping your bait warm, or are you relying on your gadgets and expensive advertising and concessions to bring you business?

Here's another good story about selling. Have you ever worked in retail? I did for a while. I worked in a toy store during the Christmas holidays one year while I was in high school, so I can relate to some of the challenges of helping retail customers.

Well, there was this young guy right out of high school who went to work for a fantastic department store. Now, it's not your normal department store; it was like Penney's and Dillard's and Cabella's and Wal-Mart and an auto mall all wrapped into one. Everything you could possibly imagine was there. The owner took an interest in all of the new employees. So the owner came down from the office and introduced himself to the kid and said, "Well, I hope you have a good first day." Then he went back up to the office.

At the end of the day, the owner went downstairs to see how the kid had done. He said, "Well, kid, how did you do today? How many customers did you help today?"

And the kid said, "Well, I … I helped one customer today."

The owner started getting red in the face, "You were here all day, and you helped *one* customer? What did you sell him?"

"Well, I sold him a fishing hook." (I like fishing stories; you can tell!)

So the owner said, "You sold him a fishing hook?"

The kid said, "Yes, and then after that, we found out he didn't have a rod and reel, so we went over and picked him out the latest new reel with the luxury rod and got him a whole big tackle box full of all of the stuff he'd need."

"Okay, that's good," the owner said. "Is that all you sold him?"

"No, no," said the kid. "We found out he didn't have any outdoor clothes, so we went over to the outdoor clothes department and got him waders and a big coat and some camo gear, while we were at it, and some new boots. He looked real sharp. And then we found out he didn't have a fishing boat, so we went over to the boat department and picked him out a beautiful boat that was going to be just right for what he wanted to do. But he didn't have a trailer, so we had to add a trailer to that. And then we found out that he drove over here this morning in his little Volkswagen Jetta and couldn't haul anything with it. So we went over to the truck department and got him a new GMC 3500 dual wheel, on-demand four-wheel drive, super torque, and he drove off."

By this time the owner's jaw was to the ground, and he was thinking he needed to find out more. He said, "This is incredible!

You sold all of this to a guy who came in looking for a fishing hook?"

And the kid said, "Well, actually, I was working in the pharmacy early this morning, and he came in looking for Band-Aids, and I happened to say to him, 'It would be a nice weekend to go fishing, don't you think?'"

If this isn't a good example of suggestive selling, I don't know what is.

How many times do you have people come in to rent a truck, and you forget to ask them about a storage unit? Or how many times do people come in to buy boxes, and you forget that they're going to need to put their boxes somewhere? You do it from time to time; you get busy and forget to take an extra second with a customer. How many times have you talked to someone on the phone and given them your store hours and then realized that you've hung up without asking them if they needed a storage unit? Don't let it happen again. You are giving away money every time you do that.

Take these silly stories and find some more that you like and share them with your people—because all of these stories help people get the mindset of being in selling mode all of the time and being "on" with their sales techniques. This allows you, then, to track things like personal bests.

Do you even have legends in your company about the day that someone rented ten units to the same company or when so-and-so rented twenty-seven units in a day? There are fantastic feats of selling that happen in your company. Find them! Celebrate them!

Have some fun with them! Some of them are really admirable, and they're just fun to think about.

Look for those wonderful feats of salesmanship. There have been people who have come into your office and were mad at you about something, and you ended up renting them a unit anyway. There have been people who went to rent from the competitor after talking to you and then showed up the next day with their stuff because they moved out of the competitor to come back to you. Stories like this are wonderful stories to tell.

Cultures also have rules. There are rules in selling. Some are unwritten, and some may already be up on the wall in your property. What kind of written and unwritten rules do you have in your selling culture?

One rule might be to get up from the desk and come around the counter to greet people when they come in to your store. One rule might be if you have two people at the counter you're dealing with and the phone rings, you let it ring to PhoneSmart instead of trying to talk on the phone and in person at the same time. That was a quick plug for PhoneSmart. Sorry about that.

Another great rule, perhaps the oldest rule of selling, is "Close early and often." If someone calls you up and says, "Do you have any storage units?" do you say, "Sure! How soon would you like to move in with us?" If you do, that is great! If the first words out of your mouth are a closing question, you are fantastic.

How do you establish selling rules in your culture? Do you write them down? Do you practice them? Do you drill them?

A selling culture also uses customer incentives, promotions, and giveaways deliberately. It's not a bad idea to always give something away to bring in business. It doesn't have to be of great value. It doesn't cost you much to buy your low-end locks, but it does bring you some goodwill if you give those away every now and then. And sometimes it doesn't matter what you give away.

A sales culture also finds a way to make its location a destination for its customers. What do you have that makes people stop in? I know a storage operator who always has fresh cookies out on the counter. He has people he hasn't rented to in years stop by to get cookies when they're out running around town. His customers stop in the office just to have a snack. Whatever it takes for you to make your store a destination for people will help you build your business.

Another way to establish and develop your sales culture is to follow your scripting. A lot of people don't like scripts. That is because a lot of people do not develop good scripts or use them correctly. Let me suggest how to use scripting properly.

Scripting should never be paragraphs; scripting should be phrases or easily digestible sentences. Salespeople have to be able to express the gist of your scripting in their own words. If you have your people memorize some fantastic phrases for qualifying questions and closing questions and let them fill in all of the rest with their normal conversation, it will turn out as friendly, concerned conversation. If you want your people to do word-for-word scripting in sentences and paragraphs, they won't be able to do it. They'll trip over it. They'll sound canned. They'll sound uncomfortable, and they'll chase your prospects away. Instead, master phrases. Master certain questions, and let that be your scripting.

When developing your script, concentrate on hitting specific points, crossing certain thresholds, and asking for the business. This can be done many different ways. When your salespeople hit the key points, cross the thresholds, and ask for business in a way that sounds conversational, you will make a lot more sales and create a lot more referrals.

Another great rule of selling is to stay away from the word "if." Say "when" instead. Don't tell your prospect, "Well, if you rent from us, you'll find that it's a great experience." Say, "When you're one of our tenants, you'll like staying here because ..." Do the assumptive selling.

We'll deal more with how to assume the sale later. If you can do that well in your organization, you will find your selling culture will thrive.

Learning to close a sale is also key to building your selling culture. Use your "alternate-choice close." Are you familiar with the alternate-choice close as a standard selling technique? You actually know it. You walk into a store to look for an item, and the sales clerk says, "Did you want that in red or green?" You go to the restaurant and hear, "Smoking or nonsmoking?" Your kids want to go to the movies; they say, "Hey, Dad, let's go to the movies! They've got a show at seven and one at nine. Which one do you want to go to?" You use it every day, and other people use it on you every day. It's powerful stuff. Teach it to your people and learn it and use it all of the time. Self-storage has many excellent alternate choices built into it. There are climate-controlled and regular units, first floor or upper floor, five-by-ten or ten-by-ten, and so on.

You should also seek out good examples of selling cultures and talk about them with your staff. Photo studios are a good example of a great selling culture. When was the last time you took your family to a photo studio to get family pictures taken? These people are great! How many times have you walked in there thinking, "Mmm, I'll probably spend x dollars on a package"? And how many times have you actually walked out having spent what you intended to spend? It's always two or three times more, isn't it? Always. And aren't you happy that you did it? Were you mad afterward? Or if you were mad, it lasted a second or two until Grandma saw the pictures and went, "Ohhhh!" Right? How do they do it? They do assumptive selling. You show up, and they know you're not there to look at a picture and go home; you're there to buy pictures. So everything they do is assumptive selling.

Photographers are masters of the alternate-choice close. They take several different poses, and then they show you the pictures and they say, "Of Pose A, which is your favorite picture? Is it this picture or that picture?" You pick one, and they put it to the side. "Let's look at Pose B; which one do you like best there, number one, two, or three?" You go, "Well, I don't like number three. "Okay, let's forget three. How about number one or two? Number two looks good, doesn't it?" "Yes, it does." "Okay, great!" Now you've got another one. And they go through every pose until they've alternate-choice closed you into a seven-page package. You can't say no. Are you going to say, "No, I don't want gorgeous pictures of my lovely children!"? You can't say it; well, some people can, but saying no is very hard—especially when your kids are sitting right next to you and listening to you. These people in the photo studio business are masters of a selling culture.

And then they've got seventeen different payment options. So if you try to get out of it by saying, "Well, you know, I don't have that much with me …," they'll say, "Oh, well, no problem! You can do this option, this option, or the other option." They're masters of both the art and science of selling.

Look at other businesses that you deal with that are masters of the selling culture, and then think about how well you master it at your store. Are you really mastering it, or are you just kind of skating? Take a look and see what you think.

As you develop your culture, you will face challenges. How do you find people to participate in your culture? I mentioned a bit about the hip-hop culture. You can't join the hip-hop culture unless you like booming bass. If you don't like your head vibrating from the bass line, you may need to find another style of music to love. Every culture has its prerequisites, which can't be ignored.

So let's talk about selling culture. How do you filter out the people who don't belong? Perhaps you have tried to train someone who wasn't really interested in being in a selling culture, and you had a bad experience. You probably did not establish the prerequisites and limit your hiring accordingly.

Let's look for some qualifying hoops. How do you find the people who you hire? If you're using advertisements, how do you word those advertisements? What do you call your position? Is your position for a salesperson? Is your position for a store manager? Whatever you call it now, I urge you to call it something different in your next advertising campaign and change it yet again in the next one. Keep playing with wording and find out what sort of people are attracted by the different ads you run for the position. It's very interesting to find out what happens.

We do this when we hire at PhoneSmart. Sometimes we call the PhoneSmart rep's job a call center position. Sometimes we call it inbound sales and sometimes marketing. We try many different things just to see what people are attracted to, and it's fascinating.

You should also do a voice screening for prospective employees. Do you hate hiring because you have to talk to seventy-five people to get two that you want to interview? It's frustrating, isn't it? So, what's the first way that people judge your staff? Let's say potential customers are calling on the phone; how much time do you think your staff has to make a great impression on the caller? Five seconds? Ten seconds? Why not set up voice mail, so your prospective hires leave a message? Your greeting will invite them to talk to you for a minute and tell you something about themselves. You give them five seconds, and if they have a smile in their voice, and you enjoy how they sound, call them up for a telephone interview. If not, delete the message and move on to the next one. It's kind of coldhearted, but your customers don't give your people more than five or ten seconds to impress them. So, use that as a yardstick.

Certainly look for the red flags and the green flags. What are those? They can be all kinds of different things. Some people don't like hiring candidates who've had lots of jobs, but I would caution you not to automatically eliminate someone because of that. Sometimes what you see is a progression of responsibility. The candidate has a goal to reach a certain level, and he or she keeps having to move through organizations to get to that level. So just because someone's had a lot of jobs doesn't mean he or she goes to work the first week and then oversleeps every day and gets fired. You have to look a little deeper into the reasons they moved from job to job. One good way to find out if the person was difficult to work with is to ask two questions. 1. Can you tell me about your worst boss and what was he or she like? 2. Can you tell me about your best boss and what he or she was like? The answers to these questions will also tell you how this person likes to be managed.

Green flags should come up with people that are fun to talk to, people you enjoy visiting with. Now, I would caution you not to hire your friends because that can be complicated. You should hire people you enjoy talking to without knowing them previously because your customers will enjoy talking to them, too. Hire people who make a great first impression on you.

There are also ways you can secret shop your potential recruits. If you're looking at a resume and you see where they're working, especially if it's a retail shop, go down there and try to buy something and see how you're treated. It will tell you tons. Call the prospect on the phone. Ask some questions about whatever the business he or she works for is. Find out how you're treated. It will tell you all you need to know. It may seem a little secret agent-ish, but it's going to save you a lot of time and trouble. Having the right person working at your property will make a huge difference to you. You already know that, don't you? It's just a matter of finding those people.

What does work history tell you? I don't know; I'm not a huge fan of resumes. I have to apologize to the educational system and people who create resumes. They're interesting, they're a way to spark some conversation, but they don't necessarily tell you what that person is capable of. They say nothing about what your candidates can do in a pinch or if they can think on their feet. You've got to find that out some other way. Test for these abilities.

I like to boil this whole process of bringing people into your sales culture down to two acid tests, because these are the two acid tests that you have to pass on a day-to-day basis at your store. When it's busy and you're tired and you're short staffed, how do you handle these situations? These are the killer phrases:

Someone calls you up on the phone and says, "How late are you open today?" If your response to that is not something like, "What time did you want to come in to rent a storage unit," you're sunk. If your response is, "Oh, we're open until six. See you later!" and you hang up, you will fail in your efforts to build a selling culture.

The next killer phrase is, "That's a little more than I'm looking to spend." When people use this line, they're determining whether they can negotiate pricing with you. They want to know if you have confidence in your pricing. If you don't, they will think you're charging too much and ripping them off. So the issue of pricing is a lot like a poker game. If your response to the more-than-I'm-looking-to-spend line is, "Oh, sorry the price is kind of high I guess," you're sunk! How your people answer the price concern also determines whether you rent to enough people in the could-go-either-way category. If you are unsure of how to handle the price discussion, keep on reading.

If the people you hire are able to deal with these killer phrases on a busy day when they're tired and short staffed, you've got the right people.

We can use PhoneSmart as a case study for a moment. We use a voicemail message for prospective hires with great success. When someone calls in response to a help-wanted ad, we've set up a greeting that tells a lot about what we do, a lot about what we're looking for, and invites callers to tell us about themselves. When listening to the callers on the employment hotline, we usually give them about five or ten seconds. If you can hear them smiling, if they're having fun with it—because a lot of times, it's embarrassing for them—then we keep listening. They don't realize that, when they call you, they're doing an audio audition until they get the message. So you get some fun stuff. It will catch some people off guard, and you can hear how good they are at recovery. If we like what we hear, we save the message and call them back to set up a telephone interview.

It's interesting that sometimes when you call the people back who sounded great on the message, they answer their phone at the house with a curt, "What?" When that happens, we're quick to say, "Oops. Sorry!" and get off the phone. When you call prospective hires back, you catch them being themselves, and you can hear if they have good speaking skills, if they can think on their feet, and if they can improvise. Those are all fantastic talents for a new staff person to have.

It's also important to hire people who have the natural tendency to be patient and friendly because, when it's slow at your store, anybody could handle the customers—no problem. But when it gets busy, your staff people need to maintain their composure and act in a friendly and professional manner with everyone. You do experience very slow times and very busy times at your stores. We see this in our call volume reports. No one in the whole country wants to rent a storage unit for one or two hours, and then everybody in the country wants one at the same time. You get that at your store, too. You'll sit there with your chin in your hand for a while, like the Maytag man, and then all of a sudden you've got five people at the counter, and the phone won't stop ringing. So how do you test to see if prospective hires can stay friendly and patient in a pinch like this?

One of the tests we've come up with to measure a candidate's composure and patience is "The Break Room Test." When someone comes in for a live interview, we sit them in the break room for a few minutes.

We say to them, "I'm sorry, the person who's interviewing you is just running a little bit late. She'll be right there." And then we'll leave the person in there for five or ten minutes. One of the staff people will walk through and just in passing say, "Hello," and if the potential hire doesn't respond in a friendly way, that's a short interview. If the person in the break room starts getting impatient and annoyed, that's a short interview. We leave some reading materials about our company and about storage in the break room. If the person being tested leafs through the material, then we feel good about their curiosity and their ability to use downtime to learn something they might need.

I can't tell you how many times we've saved ourselves from a bad hire by doing this. You might agree that a lot of people interview very well, and then after you've had them on staff for a couple of weeks, you think it's a different person or sometimes even their evil twin working for you. Our break room test is a way that you can find people who are patient and friendly, even in a pinch.

Put yourself in your candidate's position. Job interviews stink! They're terrible to go to because you never know what the people doing the hiring are looking for. You're worried about whether the interviewer(s) will like you. It's a pressurized situation, where you can see if a candidate can maintain his or her friendliness and patience under stress.

In the positions you fill and the positions we fill, people have to use computers and phones. So we run potential hires through a little test to make sure they can talk, type, and read at the same time. You might think that everyone can do basic keyboarding, manage basic software, and use a piece of telephone equipment. But not everyone can. You need to know that you have people at the store who can run your management software and fix the gate interface when it's down and know how to roll up a door without jamming it. So you have some skills you need to test for, too.

Of course, you have to test for selling skills. Hopefully you have recognized some good selling and questioning skills in the phone interview. But you need to know that the prospective hire can sell your products and services. The oldest, silliest, but still effective way of testing someone's selling skills is to grab the thing nearest to you and ask them to sell it to you. "Okay, why don't you just sell me this box of Tic Tacs." Or "How would you sell me this pen?" You put people in a terribly uncomfortable spot, and you'll see how they sell under pressure.

What you'll find is there are a lot of people who have great natural selling skills; they'll start asking you questions and trying to determine how best to approach you. When a candidate does that, you have somebody you can work with.

And then there are some people who have backward selling skills. They think that what they have to do to sell something is hit you over the head with whatever they are selling: "These are great

Tic Tacs. You need them. You should buy them." That's probably not the approach you want. You need to think about what hoops your potential hires need to jump through before you are comfortable letting them be responsible for your multimillion-dollar asset.

And, of course, seeing is believing. I definitely recommend, if you're not doing it now, that you hire people on a probationary period. Use prospective employees on a temporary project. Hire them on a test basis. See what happens. Give them a chance to get a feel for your organization because being in the storage business is not for everyone. Being a retail salesperson is not for everyone. Storage managers have to wear a lot of hats. They have to be good at selling, collecting, and operating the facility, and they have to be good at cleaning. Just because someone's good at wearing one or two of the hats doesn't mean he or she is good at wearing enough of them to be a valuable member of your staff. So set a temporary assignment with potential employees or start them part-time.

Give them increasing responsibility as they pass the day-to-day tests. Bring them on slowly so you don't overwhelm them in the beginning because, no matter what your new position is, it's overwhelming in the beginning. Usually, at the end of the first week, your new employees are in a fog, and you need to give them a day or two to settle down from that. Starting slowly also allows you to avoid committing to something that you're going to need to wiggle out of later. It's better to have a set probationary period so, if the hire doesn't work out, you have a graceful exit. You can simply decline to make a permanent offer.

If you still like the hire after the probationary period, it's much better to be able to say, "Do you know what? I'm happy I hired you. This is working great. Are you happy here, too?" You don't want to be put in the position where you hire someone off the bat on a permanent basis and then find out in thirty days you shouldn't have hired this person. Then you have to fire them. That's not fun.

Pay attention to where you're going to take the people you hire because the sky is the limit. Some people have a lot more potential in them than you see in the first couple weeks. Be prepared to develop them. Give them tasks that are interesting to them. Let them develop themselves. That's how great salespeople become great salespeople. They are given the latitude to develop. So if you see someone who has that potential, let him or her develop. Later on, you can have the employee train the next level of new people.

But be cautious about how you judge your new hires. I'll give you a good example. We almost fired a fantastic rep of ours, and here's what happened. She aced the initial testing. She did the initial training program well. She was a college student, and we were going to have her work in the evenings. Unfortunately, after a month or so on the regular schedule, her numbers just weren't that good. We couldn't figure it out because she knew what to do, and she had the personality; and we thought we may have made a hiring mistake. Sometimes with college students, work is their fifth or sixth priority in life, and that is not always acceptable to you as the employer. We thought letting her go would be too bad because she seemed to have the right stuff for us.

That next weekend, we needed to cover a Saturday morning shift. We called her up and asked, "Can you come in and work Saturday?" She came in, and she did great! We were thinking, well, Saturdays are always good, but they're not that good. Something funny is going on here. We thought perhaps it was a fluke. We asked her about it, and she said to us, "You know, I'm so glad you called me in because I really like the morning. I'm a morning person. I'm really awake in the morning. By the time I get to work here at 5:00 in the afternoon, I'm pooped. I just can't concentrate."

We never knew she was a morning person! You can't have a morning person working an evening shift after she is tired from the day; that doesn't work. So we moved her to mornings, and she did very well. Had we not known that we had her working in conflict to her body clock, we would have let a good employee go.

Here are some basic guidelines. You've heard these from everybody, but it's worth knowing again that it's the *person* who sells the storage unit. It's the attitude that sells the storage unit. So hire someone who has a great attitude and some spark and some fire in his or her eye. You can train someone to do all of the duties, but you can't train someone to have fun dealing with people. That's just something a person either has or doesn't have. So look for those kinds of people. Put them on, test them, increase their responsibility, and your selling culture will start to develop itself. As you bring in these talented people, they'll bring in their own stories and myths and legends and really help you build your sales culture.

Getting good employees into your selling culture is the first step. The next step is keeping them long enough to start increasing their responsibility. The beginning stages of a recruit's career with you are significant. There are thresholds that people hit that you may or may not be aware of. There are several important thresholds that come up early on, particularly at two weeks, two months, and six months when your employees are reevaluating their decision to stay. They ask themselves, "Did I make the right choice by coming on board here? Is this something I want to do? Am I doing the things I like? Am I getting what I need here?" These are times when you need to spend a few minutes with them, check in with them and see what's happening in their minds. The very fact that you are checking in will give them an opportunity to voice concerns.

Keep the new people challenged, because the worst thing you can do is let a talented and motivated person get bored. That's bad for two reasons. They will stop enjoying the newness of the position, and they will feel awkwardly underutilized.

Look at some of your current successes. Even if you have not been trying to build selling culture, you have had successes in your business. Who's really doing well for you and why? Some of you may have no idea why some of your best people are some of your best people. Try and figure that out. It may be you just got lucky and hired somebody with a great personality who is eager to learn and likes a challenge. Or maybe you did something, intentionally or unintentionally, to help develop them. So find out what it is you did to help these people be successful and try and do that with the next group of people.

You should start thinking today who your next good hire is going to be. I run into some good retail people from time to time, and I take note where they work and what their names are in case I have an opening, and I need to go find them again. Not every position will be appropriate for the people you run into. But when you have a position that could be a good match, your recruiting efforts could be vastly simplified.

I have been asked before: If you find a great potential employee, do you make room in the organization for them? I'd say you have to answer that question in a couple of ways for yourself. This depends a lot on your management style. Whether you like to manage a week or two ahead of the wave or a week or two behind the wave is going to determine somewhat whether you bring the new person on board before you really need him or her or whether you wait until you have an opening.

If you have a weak player who you need to replace, I would say to bring the new person on as a temporary. Give him or her some temporary assignments to make sure the prospect will work out, and then allow the weaker person on the team to go find new employment. That way you could be sure you have a strong replacement before you let the weak employee go.

But if everybody on your team is doing well, and you've found someone who you think is outstanding, if you make room for that person, you'll have increased your payroll costs. Can you justify doing so? Are you going to get enough return from that person's work to justify the increase in your expenses? You may gain more benefits than you anticipated by bringing on a good new person. He or she may find many ways to bring value to your selling culture that you could not have planned. You have to ask yourself if the potential gain is worth the additional payroll.

One of the challenges we have in self-storage, as you know, is that the business can be somewhat seasonal. So there are times that we're hiring people, and there are times when we're letting people go. Can you keep a good potential recruit waiting while you wait out the seasonal changes?

There certainly are challenges involved in hiring good people because it's true that good help is hard to find. It's not just a myth. It's also true that what our business offers people is not for everyone, and you just have to realize that. Sometimes you have to let nice people go because the position you are trying to fit them into is just not for them. You might feel bad about letting the person go. But it's nicer and smarter for you to let someone go if the job isn't for him or her. It is not a good idea to keep unhappy people on and torture them or to let your revenues and your customers suffer.

There is an interesting fact about wages: the money is not as important as you think. I hear a lot of people at trade shows ask each other, "What do you pay your manager?" I realize you have to pay people something. Your employees have to make enough to make it worth it to them to get up each day and go to work. They have to feel as though they are getting fair market value for the time, effort, and energy they put into growing your business. But do you know what? An extra dollar or two an hour doesn't make a bit of difference to someone who is bored or not challenged or who doesn't like what he or she is doing.

So remember that the main motivator for employees is feeling valued and feeling as if they contribute value. If people like what they're doing and like the way you deal with them and like the challenge involved in the job, an extra dollar or two an hour is not going to make a difference to them. So don't be so hung up on exactly what their wages are; be more hung up on how interested and engaged your employees are. Be more concerned about how much they enjoy their interaction with you, how well they take direction from you, and how well they give feedback to you. Those are good indicators of how your selling culture is building and how it's coming together.

So now I challenge you to go out and finish building your selling culture. I would like you to do something right now. Write down two things you are going to implement today to help build your sales culture. It's wonderful to read about methods or to go to seminars and get some tips and some ideas. But if you don't implement any of them, then I am not sure I have brought you any value. I've enjoyed spending time writing about building a selling culture, in any case, but I would like to run into you some time and hear you say, "Do you know what? Because of how you made me think, I did this and I did that, and here are the results I got. Thank you." So make a note: what are the two things you're going to do to move your selling culture forward?

Sales 101:
Learning the Basics of Sales

Now that you're ready to get your selling culture moving in the right direction, you will need some specific instruction on the art and science of sales. Some of this may seem like the same old speech on sales that you have heard before. But chances are you need to hear it again. If you play sports, you know that you need to always work on your game and review fundamentals. Why should sales be any different?

In this section, I hope to bring you some basic selling skills that you can use no matter what you sell, no matter what you do, because you are always selling something—if only just yourself, your ideas, your desires, your products, or your services. So "Sales 101" should teach you some of the basic sales skills that successful salespeople use every day.

The first rule of selling is this: You can't sell anyone anything. You can, however, help people talk themselves into buying just about anything.

Read the first rule of selling again. No, really, go back a few lines and read it again.

If this rule is true, then learning to sell is all about helping people talk themselves into buying from you. Okay, read on.

The first step in sales is the introduction. Now, you hear some sort of an introduction anytime you walk into a store or make a phone call to a business: "Hello, how are you? How can I help you? Thanks for calling. My name is Joe. What can I do for you?"

An introduction is very important but maybe not for the reasons you think. You might think the introduction's purpose is to brand the business, or to tell the caller or the visitor something about what differentiates you. Not so. A good greeting gives you a chance to smile with your prospect. Notice I did not say smile *at* your prospect. Smile *with* your prospects. The power in a greeting is in a shared smile. You want potential customers to hear you smile and see you smile; people want a friendly exchange with someone. They want to share a smile with someone. Make it happen.

How many times have you gone into a store, and the retail person on the other end of the counter looked at you with a bored or even annoyed look and said, "Hello," and that was it? How much fun was that? How many times have you made a phone call to a business, and it was clear to you that you interrupted the person from whatever they were doing, and you got a frown, a gruff, or even a grump? How fun was that? No fun at all! What was your buying mood at that point? Let's not do that to our prospects! Smile. Say hello. Use your name if you want; don't use your name if you don't want to. It doesn't matter. The whole point of the introduction is to share a smile with people during their first seconds of being in your space.

A good smile breaks the ice, releases the tension, and tells your prospects that you are a real person who values their time and their feelings and their money. Yes, all that happens in just one good smile. I don't care what you say in your introduction as long as it is not ridiculous or long-winded. You've got to say it with a smile, and you have to mean the smile when you give it. An insincere smile is worse than none at all.

Now that you have a good greeting that is going to give your prospects a smile and put them in the mood to listen to you, let's get on with helping them talk themselves into buying from you.

The next thing you need to do in any kind of selling situation is to ask some good discovery questions. Wait a minute, you say. Why are you asking questions? Shouldn't you be selling something? No! You can't sell people something by rattling at them and telling them about this feature and that feature; you'll be going on and on about stuff that probably doesn't mean anything to them anyway. That's not how you sell to people. It's certainly not how you help people talk themselves into buying from you. That's how you get people to walk out of your store, or even worse, that's how you get them to close off their minds to you.

How you sell to people is to ask them some good qualifying questions. For instance: Why did you pick up this book? What are you looking for in sales training? What techniques do you try that don't work for you? When have you been frustrated when trying to make a sale? Those are discovery questions.

So what you need to do is to find what questions work well for what you are selling. How many times have you walked into a clothing store and the retail person has said, "Can I help you to-day?" That's not a qualifying question; that's an invitation for you to say, "No, I'm just looking, thanks" and shut off the whole process. How many times have you walked into a retail shop, and the person has said to you, "Hi! Are you shopping for yourself, or are you looking for a gift for someone else today?"

Well, how do you get away from that one? You can't just go, "Never mind. I'm just looking." It isn't that easy. You're now in a conversation. You have to say, "Well, my mother-in-law has a birth-day coming up, and I have no idea what to buy for her, and I'd better buy her something because she did something really nice for me a couple of weeks ago." Oh, my gosh! Now the salesperson knows what you want and how to help you. That's why you ask good discovery questions. There is no other way to know how to help your prospect talk him or herself into buying. So figure out what discovery questions work well for what you're selling and then learn to listen.

The best salespeople sell because they listen. If you listen, the prospects are going to tell you why they're interested in what you have to offer and why they're not interested in what you have to offer, and then you have someplace to go in your conversation. You have some way of knowing what the conversation is going to be.

So, ask your questions and listen. Hear what prospective cus-tomers are saying. People will give you buying signs. A buying sign is something like, "Well, I was thinking about getting a Budweiser mug because I just love the Budweiser horse ads." My gosh, there's a buying sign for you. Take that person to the beer mug section of the store and sell him or her a Budweiser mug. Listen for buying signs.

Also listen for concerns that the person might have. The person might say, "Well, I really would like a new suit, but, you know, I just don't think I can get it this paycheck, unless I can find a real bargain." Well, okay, now you know that if you can find this person something on the sale rack that's going to look like it didn't come off the sale rack, he can get it on this paycheck and not the next paycheck. You get credit for a sale today. The customer gets to look good now for less money than he had hoped he'd spend. The store gets to clear out inventory and add revenue. Everyone wins! So listen to what people are telling you.

During your discovery-question phase of your sales process, you also have the chance to raise some important considerations. While you're listening to people talk, you're able to think about their situation and raise considerations that they normally would not have thought about. For instance, if someone is shopping for a self storage unit to put Grandma's antiques in storage, they might not know air-conditioned storage exists. Maybe they're scared to death to put that antique in storage because they don't want all of the joints to get out of whack. In your role as the storage professional, you explain that you have a climate-controlled unit in which the temperature will not get above 80 degrees, and the humidity stays under control. Now this person is thinking, *Oh, thank goodness! There's a solution for me.* Remember to raise some important considerations for people. You know your business; they do not.

Your discovery questions will also allow you to qualify the prospect. Does the prospect qualify to buy this product? If you're selling a car you need to know if your prospect has a driver's license. Does she know how to drive? Does he have money to buy the car? There are basic qualifications that you need to get past when you're trying to sell to anyone. In your discovery-question phase, you can find out: Does this person have the means? Does this person have the authority? Is this sale going to happen if I can prove the value of the purchase and satisfy all of the concerns that might block the sale? So your discovery questions are very important to determine not only if you have a genuine prospect in front of you but to also determine how this prospect will decide to buy.

Your discovery questions tell you where your prospect falls in your Rule of Thirds theory. Is this going to be a gimme? Is there no way a sale is going to happen any time soon? Is this a sale you are going to have to work for?

Your discovery questions are also going to allow you to build agreement with that person, and that's what selling is all about. No matter what you're selling, there are certain issues you have to agree on before the whole deal can come together, and the discovery questions help you build agreement.

For instance, if I were selling puppy dogs, and you came to me looking for a puppy dog, one of the questions I might ask you is, "What breed do you like?" And if you don't want the breed that I'm selling, we've got problems. There are very basic issues in every sale that you have to build agreement on.

For instance, if you came to me because you wanted to rent a self-storage unit, I need to know when you need the unit. If you don't need it pretty soon, I'm not going to rent you one any time this month. If you don't know where my self-storage location is or how to get there, or if it's not convenient for you to get to, I'm not going to rent you a unit. Do you know what size you need? Can I help you figure a size? Do we actually have a size that is going to meet your needs? If we can't agree on these issues, I'm not going to rent you a storage unit.

No matter what you're selling, there are certain topics and issues you and your potential customer have to agree on. Find out what those topics are, build some questions that will help you come to agreement on those topics, and go from there.

Pretend you're buying clothes at my retail shop. You need a new dress for Saturday night. You and your girlfriends are going to a happening. What color do you like? What color do you think looks good on you? If we can't agree on the color of your dress, I'm not selling you a dress. What sort of a hemline do you like? Do you like a pouffe skirt? Do you want the skirt to twirl when you spin? Do you like it tight? If we can't agree on these issues, I'm not selling you a dress. So pinpoint the issues on which you need to build agreement with your customers and come up with ways to do that.

Then create urgency. How do you create urgency? Urgency means that the prospect you're selling to wants to buy now. It doesn't help you if that person buys later—if you're selling products and services, you *will* need customers later also—you need customers now. So what is it that's going to help that person buy now rather than later or not at all or not from you?

Why is it so important that the prospect buys now? Because when the mood to buy is high, resistance is low, and attention is focused on making the purchase. The prospect wants to get this item marked off his to-do list. If you let this window of high opportunity pass, then the prospect may get distracted and spend his or her money elsewhere. The prospect may find another priority that trumps your offering. Just because a prospect expresses the intent to buy from you, does not mean things won't change or other priorities won't arise.

I have wanted a new electric guitar for over a year now. I've been in a guitar store at least six times because I happened to be right by one while dong other things. But I haven't bought a guitar from any of the stores yet. Something has always distracted me from my intended purchase. Someone in one of those stores should have taken me off the market. But no one has yet. Give your prospect the satisfaction and peace of mind that an immediate purchase will bring. Give yourself the immediate revenue you need.

Let's take a look at what prospects need. You should understand that purchasing from you now is a good thing for the prospect, whether the prospect expresses some hesitation or not. What about that person who needs a dress on Saturday? If it's Monday, she needs to buy the dress now because she will need to make sure she can get the right shoes and the right hose and the right accessories. If she waits until Thursday or Friday to buy that dress, and it doesn't fit quite right, she's in trouble. You see she needs to get the dress now so that she can get everything else in place by Saturday. If you let her walk out of the store without a dress, you are doing her a disservice. She will be stressed out the rest of the week worrying about the dress. And when she comes back, if she comes back, to your store on Thursday, maybe you will be sold out of her size or her color. Now you have set her up for a disaster. If you are in the fashion business, it is your job and your mission to prevent your customers and potential customers from experiencing a fashion disaster.

I am not joking around. It's your job to prevent the fashion crisis. If you see every prospect walking into your dress shop as a person you can save from a fashion meltdown, you will be sure to give each customer an excellent fashion solution in plenty of time for whatever event is coming up. Every time you let a prospect walk out without a good fashion solution in his or her shopping bag, you have thrown someone to the fashion wolves to be mercilessly ravaged. Why would you do that to someone?

If someone is looking to rent a storage unit from your self-storage place, and it's your busy season, the prospect needs to rent from you now because you don't know what you're going to have available tomorrow. Whatever you're selling, you need to find a way to build some urgency for that person. Limited availability, limited time, limited opportunity—these are things that help people decide, "I'm going to buy now." If they think it's urgent, they will think they need to do something about the situation now. They need a little nudge to say yes to the deal.

How do you, then, close the deal? Well, let's talk a little bit about the concept of closing. I don't know if you use the term the same way I would use the term in selling. Closing a call, closing a deal, is not saying, "Thanks for coming by; hope you buy from us." That's not closing. Closing is getting the signature on the deal or on the contract—getting the check, getting the payment; that is closing the deal.

Now some people say that using the word "close" sounds kind of harsh. It sounds like someone might get hurt. I've heard it said that you should think about making a sale as if you were opening up a new friendship, opening a new account, or starting a new business relationship. This is a nice way of looking at it.

I still like the word "close" because it's the point where one relationship ends and another begins. This person is no longer your prospect after "the close." He is now your customer or your client. So you are closing an old chapter in your relationship. You are no longer the potential vendor. You are now the vendor/consultant/ expert of choice. You are also closing the conversation. There is no longer any need to discuss the black dress for Saturday night. Everything has been decided. You can now close the conversation and complete the transaction. The customer can close her internal discussion of the purchase. There is no longer any need to fret about Saturday. The outfit has been decided. All is well. It is time to devote thought and energy to something else.

So, how do you close? Well, you have to ask questions that lead you to the "big yes." The "big yes" is, "Yes, I'll take this dress." "Yes, I'll rent that ten-by-ten storage unit." "Yes, I'll buy that puppy." That's the "big yes" you're leading to. Your discovery questions and your agreements help you get to "yes" because, every time potential customers agree with you on a small topic, a minor issue, or a simple concern, they're building to the "big yes." Each time you and the prospects agree on something, there are fewer things that will get in the way of their pending decision to buy now.

You should be constantly asking well thought out and pertinent questions that help close the sale all the way through the process. The most popular close is "the alternate-choice"; and, as I pointed out earlier, whether you know it or not, you've had it used on you a million times, and you've used it a million times. "Well, let's go to the movies. Do you want to go Saturday, or do you want to go

Friday?" "Gee, I really like that outfit. Should I get it in brown, or should I get it in red?" You hear the alternate choice close being used all day long. The first question that a car salesman might ask you when you walk into the showroom is, "Would you like stick or would you like automatic?" The alternate-choice close rules all selling situations. It is so good because it helps the prospect make decisions, which all lead to buying from you. It creates a decision tree that the prospect can organize in his or her mind to go through all the options, small decisions, and minor considerations involved in making the big decision to buy now. So use the alternate-choice whenever you can.

Figure out how you're going to do the alternate-choice for your business. If you're burning CDs or DVDs for a living, you could ask if you should pack them in the jewel case or the paper case. Use your alternate-choice. It works every time.

Let's look at the concept called "closing on the minor issues." This is what building agreements is all about, and this is an easy way to build to the "big yes." If I were selling you widgets, and I found out that you take five hundred widgets a week, you like them on Tuesdays and Thursdays, you prefer them packed in grease rather than packed in bubble wrap, by the time we get through our discussion, we've already agreed on every minor issue involved in the sale, and the only thing left for me to do is hand you the pen and say, "Let me have your approval. I'll start you up next week." Every sale has many minor issues that can be resolved, which will lead to the sale.

In self-storage, there are many minor issues as well. Will the new renter need climate control? What sort of lock should your prospect choose? How will prospects get their belongings to the storage unit? Do they want to pay by check or credit card?

Look for any minor issues involved in your product and service and figure out good ways to get agreement on each of them.

Another classic close is called "the puppy-dog close." I love it because I used to sell adult dogs and puppies. If I had a qualified prospect and I knew the people liked the breed I sold, that they had a good environment for the dog, that they had a little dog sense about them, and that they knew how to handle a dog, I would not ask for payment. I would give them a dog well suited for them, whether it was a puppy or an older dog and say, "I'll tell you what, take the dog home. If in two weeks it's not working out, I'll be glad to just take the dog back." How many dogs do you think I took back? Maybe one or two in a hundred. I had to take practically none of them back because I was careful about who I left the dog with and made sure the dog fit the situation.

The puppy dog close is so popular and effective, that some dealerships are doing it with cars now. How many of you have seen the overnight test-drive? That is the classic puppy-dog close. The salesman says, "Here are the keys to the car. Bring it back tomorrow. If it doesn't work out, no problem." How many cars do you think they're selling this way? A ton of them! Do the car dealerships do a lot of prequalifying before they let you take the car home? You bet they do.

So if you can design a puppy-dog close with your products or service, do it! How many stores do a return policy that's very simple? You can buy clothes at about any store, bring them home, wear them in front of the mirror, show them to your husband or wife, and if the clothes don't work out, you can take them back and get a full return on your purchase. It's a wonderful puppy-dog close. It is especially effective when the customer purchases with a credit card because no money changes hands until the purchase is confirmed. Find out how the puppy-dog close works for your situation and create one that works for you.

Another wonderful close is called "the order-blank close." The theory behind the order-blank close is this: If I'm filling out the order and getting all of your information, until you stop me we have a sale.

Have you ever been on the phone where the first thing the phone rep said was, "Can I please have your name … and a phone number … and an address?" And pretty soon the rep has everything he or she needs from you to write up the order, and the only thing left for him or her to do is to say, "Would you like to use Visa, MasterCard, or Discover today?"

The order-blank close works wonderfully in self-storage. All you have to do is tell the person, "Let me just get a little information from you," and start filling out your lease forms or your reservation forms. Use the order-blank close in your business. It's simple. It's low pressure. It's easy for your staff to master.

I hope you find ways to apply all of these closes to your business. In order to learn what you need to know about each prospect, and in order to be able to use any of these closes, you will need to gather good information with well-phrased questions.

You have read a lot about good questions in this book. Let's look at some specific questioning techniques. You have a couple of kinds of questions you can ask; and if you've studied sales before, you know what they are. I'm going to repeat them because they are worth repeating.

There are open-end questions. Any question that's going to be answered by an explanation is an open-ended question. You want to ask as many of these as you can in the discovery phase. You want to ask as many of these as you can while you're building agreement because you want to know as much as you can so you can know which way to take this prospect down the road to creating urgency and the close.

You're also going to ask some closed-ended questions, too. These are questions that are answered "yes" or "no." You need to ask these when you need specific information, when you need that prospect to make a clear decision about one option or another. It's a good idea to use a mix of open-ended and closed-ended questions. You have to be careful which one you use and when you use them. If you use your closed-ended questions too soon in the process, your prospect may say "no" at a critical stage in the process, and you will have shot yourself in the foot. The closed-ended questions need to sound natural in the conversation, so you have to be careful about doing correct preparation before you use them.

Many times, you can help people make decisions by paraphrasing what they just told you. Paraphrasing is a very important technique whenever you're selling because it helps you to clarify what your prospect said. It also allows the prospect to hear what was said in your words so he or she can confirm what it was that was said to you.

If you are completely lost, let's look at it from this point of view: I say, "How soon are you going to need to buy that car? Do you have any events coming up where you'd like to look sharp in your new car?" And the prospect says, "Well, I think I'd like to be in my new car by the end of the month," So I say, "Oh, so you think you'd like to be in your new car by the end of the month?" And the person says, "Yes." Now this person has committed to taking delivery by the end of the month. It will be difficult and awkward to tell me later that the car isn't needed until several months from now.

If your prospect says something, she may have been expressing her intent, or she may have just been thinking out loud. When you paraphrase and repeat the statement back to her and she confirms it, then she has made a decision. It can no longer be just an act of thinking out loud or of talking to herself. There is no way this person can say, "I don't want the car until next month" because she told you she wanted it by the end of this month. You checked with her; she confirmed it. If she says, "Oh, no, really I don't need it until Christmas," now she's stuck in a lie to herself.

You need to sell her a car this month to make your numbers. You can hold her to that schedule if she told you once and then confirmed to you once more that this is her intention. Most people won't go back on something they've confirmed to you.

If you use the paraphrasing technique to confirm information, your potential customer is going to stick with what was said. If you're trying to sell someone on renting a self-storage unit, and he says, "I think a ten-by-ten unit will work for me," and you say, "Oh, so you think the ten-by-ten will work?" and he says, "Yes, it will," now he's in a ten-by-ten.

Paraphrasing also works very well to flush out the genuine issues that are preventing a sale from happening. If you ask the prospect to make the purchase, and the prospect gives you a reason why she is not ready to buy, try this: "If I understand you correctly, you feel that ... (whatever was said)." This allows her to hear what she sounded like when she said it to you originally. Sometimes this will make the prospect think about what she said, and the reason's importance will diminish. This is especially true when buying from you seems like a good idea. When your solution meets the prospect's needs and the timing seems good, any reason to delay a buying decision might seem legitimate to the prospect when she says it. But when you say it back to her, it might not sound like such a good reason any longer, and you can overcome the reason more easily and still make the sale.

These are just a few ways paraphrasing can work well for you. You have noticed I paraphrased myself several times in writing about paraphrasing. I hope this helped drive the point home that something your prospect says once may only be a test sounding of the idea. But something your prospect says two or three times or confirms when you ask for confirmation becomes an intention.

When a prospect voices intention, he or she has made a decision to purchase. This is why your silence is often a very important part of the selling process. You must learn to be silent. It's very difficult because you're probably excited about what you're selling. You are excited about what you want. You want to get your way. You think you have one on the hook. You want to score a victory. People in sales like sales because they like the thrill of the fight and the ecstasy of the win; and if you can't get the win, you don't like it. So you get excited about that. Sometimes you talk too much or talk too fast. Sometimes you know way too much about your product or service and want to share that information all at once.

You have to be quiet. Especially when you ask open-ended questions or when you're building agreement. You have to let the prospect talk because, as you know, in reality you can't sell anybody anything. You can only help people talk themselves into buying what you're offering. They can't talk themselves into buying if all they hear is you going, "Bah, blah, blah, yada, yada." So prospective buyers have to do the talking; they have to do the mental and emotional processing; you have to do the listening.

Yes, you have to keep control of the flow of the call or the conversation—of how the sales process goes—but if customers can't talk themselves into making a purchase because they can't hear themselves think, the sale is not going to happen. So you've got to be quiet. If you're selling on the telephone, there is a very simple technique: do a physical action that keeps you from talking. Bite your lip. Bite your knuckle. Do something to stop yourself from talking.

If you're talking in person with people, come up with some sort of physical business that you can do to stop yourself from talking. Tap your toe imperceptibly, pinch your finger, grab your leg, cross your fingers, grip your pen or something. Do something to stop yourself from talking.

You do have to be a little careful how you do this so you don't get caught. I was in an upper management meeting listening intently and trying to hold my tongue. I have learned over the years to mostly hold my thoughts until the other people have finished speaking. This has not always been easy for me to do, so I try different bits of physical activity to make myself be quiet and listen carefully.

In the upper management meeting I mentioned, I was working a pencil in my hand. While someone else was talking, I snapped the pencil in two. That was an embarrassing interruption. All I could do was to apologize and laugh at myself and let everyone else get some laughter out as well to smooth over the awkwardness of the moment.

I can't say enough about how much you have to work on ways to be quiet when it is time to be quiet. That's a pretty good use of irony, isn't it?

Now that you are getting far enough into the sales process that people are talking to themselves about whether or not to buy from you, you are going to hear reasons why people are not yet ready to buy. So you will need to learn to deal with the concerns that people have.

You hear people talk about objections and rebuttals in the sales world. Those are really poor terms for what really happens. People don't object to what you're offering them. You don't have someone jump up and say, "I object to buying salsa with my chips!" Buying is not a scene depicting two lawyers slugging it out in the courtroom, objecting to each other's lines of questioning. People have concerns. They're concerned that they're spending money on something that's not going to work out. They're concerned that their friends might think they're an idiot for spending the money on something goofy. They are concerned they will make a poor decision or that you will give them a bad experience. So you have to figure out what concerns people have about your offering and how you can assure them that accepting your offering is a good move for them.

How you help people accept your offering is by understanding before you counter. If someone is raising a concern, allow him to tell you what that concern is. You may have heard this concern fifty-seven times today, buy if you cut that person off, thinking you know what he is saying, he's not going to like it. Let people finish what they have to say. Understand what they said. Try to look between the lines to understand the customer's emotional position. Use paraphrasing to help him to explain it some more, and then assure him that what you are offering is a good thing.

That's how it works. Understand before you counter. Assure your customers that their concerns are not new concerns. Show them how your offering takes these concerns into account and makes everything better.

Try "feel-felt-found." I have already told you that it's a wonderful tool that people use all of the time in selling. It has many different names, but it goes like this: "I know how you feel. A lot of our very satisfied customers felt that way at one time, too; what they found was that our solution was very well thought out and met their needs very well."

You can use the feel-felt-found in just about every selling and customer service situation you encounter. Feel with people what they're feeling. Let them know their feelings are legitimate. Let them know other people have felt that way. Maybe you even felt that way before coming to work for the company. And then tell them what folks found when they allowed the process to happen and did business with you. This strategy works quite well, especially when you have some good, real-life stories at hand to illustrate the point. Here is where references and notes of recommendation can help a whole lot, too.

Let's talk just a little bit about how you know how to sell to people you're selling to. Let's talk about the Rule of Thirds some more. The Rule of Thirds assumes that one group of people who come to you are going to do business with you no matter what (unless you drive them off) because they've already decided what you have to offer is going to work for them. Another group of people is not going to do business with you now no matter what because their situation is going to change, they're not qualified, and maybe they don't have the ability or the authority. And a third group could go either way.

Now, anyone who's halfway friendly and halfway knowledgeable will do business with the easy third. Sometimes you don't even have to be friendly or knowledgeable; you just have to know how to collect the payment. That's why fast-food companies make so much money with such unskilled labor; when you're craving a taco, you're getting a taco no matter how rude the people in the drive-through window or behind the counter are. That's just how it goes, and that's what the fast-food companies bank on. They know that one group loves tacos and is coming for their tacos no matter what. They invest their dollars in marketing, so the middle third that can go either way learns to crave their food. Your craving will make you buy, in spite of less than good customer service and in spite of the fact that you really don't love tacos that much anyway. Creating a craving is the key to good marketing for most kinds of products.

Now, on the other hand, the people who aren't looking for tacos aren't even going to make the stop. So the taco makers don't care about that impossible third for immediate business. They do try to get the impossible third to reconsider their position with ad campaigns like "think outside the bun" or "Fourth Meal."

But in every business, you make your money in that third that can go either way. These are the people who the advertising dollars are really targeting. Those people who think they might want a taco only make the taco makers money when they actually go and buy the taco. If you know how to sell—know how to ask your discovery questions and build agreement and create urgency and close the sale and help that person talk themselves into your offering—you're going to do business with a lot of people in that middle third. That's where you're going to make your money.

Look at each and every sales opportunity with the Rule of Thirds in mind. Is this person in the easy third? If they are, ask yourself, what can I do to make sure I don't chase them off?

If your prospect is in the impossible third, consider what you can do to give her a good experience so when her situation changes, she'll think of you and come to you first.

As for the rest—the middle third—you should concentrate on helping them begin to tell themselves that buying from you looks like a good idea. Don't let them go somewhere else or decide they really don't want your product anyway. The middle third is where you make your money, and how you make your money in the middle third is getting really good at Sales 101. Sales 101 brings results, and results, after all, are what we're all looking for.

Applying Sales Skills to Selling Self-Storage

Now that you have a clearer understanding of how to build your sales culture and of the basic rules, methods, and theories of sales, let's talk specifically about using Sales 101 in your self-storage business.

In this section, we're going to study selling techniques and structures that work for selling self-storage and apply them directly to the situations you find yourself in every day in the self-storage business.

The first thing I'd like to cover with you is the challenge of operational changes. If you're a store manager or a storage consultant and you're reading this, you've probably gotten these from a regional manager, from your operations director or from your owners, and you've thought, *Oh, geez, not another training program. Oh, no, not another operational directive.* I feel for you. You have probably been given many operational changes to implement and many new sales directions to take. The follow-up from your superiors has not always been very thorough. The strategies and initiatives have not always been very well thought out, either. I think you may feel that someone's giving you grief by giving you this book, which represents yet another operational shift, and you're probably right. There is a certain amount of grief involved in adopting new ideas and implementing new programs.

If you are the owner, operations manager, or regional director I was writing about in the last paragraph, I apologize for suggesting that you hatch some half-baked schemes and then don't follow through on them very well. But you often have too many irons in the fires and even some of your sensible initiatives have died for lack of resources, attention, and follow-through. Isn't that correct?

The advantage that this book will hopefully give you is that you don't have to do anything but talk about it. If you talk about the book and the ideas, suggestions, and techniques I deal with, you will find yourself using some of them and also taking a closer look at what you do and how you do it. This is all helpful to your business. Your staff, however, is probably grieving that you are now giving them more to think about, more to do, and new ways of looking at things.

I believe that there are seven steps of grief that self-storage managers go through when experiencing operational changes. Typically, the first step they go through is confusion. You confuse them. Your staff looks at you and thinks, *Oh, no, they're doing something else again. Ah, geez, what do they want from me?* I understand.

You can help them get through the confused stage by assuring them that you are trying to provide tools and skills that will help them manage the business better. You are trying to make their lives easier and more effective. This will help.

The next phase your staff will probably go through is a threatened phase. Your staff is going to feel like, *Well, geez, do they think*

I'm not doing my job? Are they setting me up to get canned? They will probably be a little threatened by the ideas in this book and the practices I am advocating. I understand. They are probably also thinking, *Hey, I've been doing this a long time. I know what I'm doing. You can't tell me how I should do things. I rent a lot of units. There are no new ideas.* New ideas and new practices always appear threatening at first.

You can help get your crew through the threatened phase by assuring them you would not invest training and education in an employee you did not have confidence in. You can tell them about some of the successes people and companies have had implementing what I suggest. This will help them feel less threatened.

The next thing you're probably going to see your people go through is a period of resistance, and that's okay. They're thinking, *What are they telling me that I don't know already? I don't really need this.* Your staff may tell you that the strategies and tactics I promote do not work. They may try something once and feel awkward about it and then tell you they will not try it again. But if you reassure people that there is additional business to gain by learning and practicing what has been successful in other businesses and in other self-storage operations, they will go along with your experiment. At first, they may go along just to humor you.

The next thing you're going to see your managers and staff go through is the tentative phase. They will come to accept that some of these ideas might be worth trying. They will say something like, "Okay, I'll try it. I'll read it. I'll listen to it. I'll put in the time. I'll give it a chance." I understand why they will act tentatively at first. I'd do the same thing if I were in their shoes and felt as if someone was giving me grief.

The next thing you'll go through is a curious phase. Your people will try a few things that work. Customers will respond in a positive manner. Your crew will begin to think, *Hmm, that's not a half bad idea. Oh, well that's one way of looking at things.*

And the next thing you know, people will begin to get a little excited. In this phase of excitement, your staff will begin to see some successes and will want to try more new ways of doing things and saying things. You may even become a little excited. You'll try one of my suggestions one day, and you'll say, "I'll be danged; it worked!" You'll get excited and try something else and say, "Hey, that worked too!" And you'll sit down and look at some of the structures I'm going to give you and say, "You know, that halfway makes sense. That is how it works when you're selling self-storage." You'll start working with this selling system, and you'll get into it; you'll use it day after day with prospect after prospect, and you'll rent more units. And you're going to love it! Then you'll experience bliss, and that's where I want you to get to.

When you have internalized and memorized the basics of selling and you use it every day without really thinking about it, you will have totally forgotten about the day when people would slip away from you for no good reason. You will have forgotten how people used to stump you, when they'd say things like: "I'm still shopping." "That's more than I'd like to spend." "I'm just shopping for prices." "Oh, I can't rent today. I need to get permission from my spouse." All of those bad memories will be gone, and you'll be in self-storage bliss.

And yes, I'm halfway goofing around with you, but the feeling you will have when you see a boost in revenue is serious. This is how the process works when people are introduced to a new initiative and start working with it. They go through phases of resistance and acceptance that you have to help them through. You can't take a staff that has never used selling styles before and expect them to wake up the next day as dynamite salespeople. Becoming sales experts is a process. So let's get started selling self-storage.

What is the structure of the sales process in selling self-storage? Hopefully, your store gets a lot of telephone inquiries, and so much of your selling is done on the phone. But the same process holds true when someone walks in the door and says, "How much is one of those storage things?"

We're not going to talk about dealing with current tenants now, so we're going to get them right off of the table. I am hoping that you and your staff already know how to be friendly and helpful to your current tenants. If you learn to sell with better effectiveness, it will automatically improve your interactions with current customers. But for the sake of keeping it simple, let's just talk about new potential renters.

The conversation will usually start one of two ways. Your prospects will either say, "How much is …" and they'll name off a unit that they think they're supposed to get, or they'll say something like, "I need to store my stuff. Help me." They're either going to ask you for a price or they're going to ask you for help.

The people who start off asking for help are great to deal with. All you have to do is act the part of the storage expert, take them by the hand, and lead them through the process. The prospects who start out the conversation asking about price can sometimes be handled in exactly the same way, but sometimes they require more thorough and more careful handling.

Basically, there are three components to our sales structure. First, we want to build agreement with the caller; if you recall from "Sales 101," agreement is what selling is about. Second, we're going to need an effective price stall; what I mean by that is, when prospective customers ask you, "How much is that unit?" if you're not ready to tell them what the price is, you've got to stall them, but you've got to stall them in such a way that they're comfortable. You can't just say, "Well, I don't want to tell you the price of that until I'm ready." That's not going to work.

Now there are also concerns that people bring up when they're looking to rent a storage unit. The third part of the structure is dealing with concerns. The typical ones are: "I'm still shopping around." "That's more than I'm looking to spend." "I need to get permission from somebody else before I can actually do this."

As to building agreement, I maintain that there are only five issues you need agreement on before you can ask some one to rent from you. The first agreement is timeframe. If you can't agree with callers that they need the unit pretty soon, you can't put one on hold for them. So, the first qualifying question you ask is, "How soon are you going to need to store with us?" or "How soon are you going to need something?" If the caller doesn't need the unit until next Christmas, your call is going to go quite differently than if he or she says, "I need it tomorrow."

The timeframe agreement goes on your thumb because, if someone needs a unit right away, you've got a "thumb's up." If a prospect needs a unit very soon, he will have tolerance for issues other than timeframe. As to price, he'll be willing to pay a little more. As to location, he'll be willing to travel a little farther. He will have tolerance for features and amenities and accept pretty much whatever you have to offer. He will also have tolerance for size and will accept a unit that is perhaps not exactly right for him because he doesn't have time to mess around. He needs to get his stuff in storage soon.

The next agreement is the convenience of your location. "Do you know where we're located?" "Have you ever been by here?" "Do you know where we are on 5th Street?" That's a very important question to ask because, if the caller or the prospect knows where you're located and says, "Yes, it's a convenient location," you're half-way home. All of the studies that everyone has ever done tell you that the reason people store someplace is because it's convenient for them to get there and use. Location is the number one reason people rent.

Location goes on your index finger because it is the number one reason people select a storage place. If your location is convenient for your prospect, that prospect will have tolerance for any and everything else.

Size is the next thing you have to agree on. Most people who've been in the storage business for more than a few minutes are great at helping people figure size, but here's one thing to consider: it's not important what size *you* think prospects should fit in; it's important what size *the callers* think they should fit in. And it doesn't matter what you agree on as long as it's close. If that person really needs a ten-by-fifteen, but they agree they need a ten-by-ten, you're going to show them a ten-by-ten and a ten-by-fifteen when they come down anyway. Now if they need a five-by-five, and you agree they need a ten-by-twenty, well, that's a different story. But as long as you're close, coming to an exact agreement doesn't matter. I once made a secret shop to a storage facility where the manager argued with me for five minutes over what size I needed. What a waste.

"Mrs. Caller, it sounds like you might fit in a ten-by-ten or maybe a ten-by-fifteen. If you can visualize your belongings in one of those sizes, which one do you think might work best for you?"

The caller says, "Hmm, probably the ten-by-fifteen."

Great! Hold a ten-by-fifteen. Show a couple of other sizes when the caller comes down just to make sure she has what she needs.

Agreement on size is the third agreement, and it goes on your middle finger because size does matter, but only in helping you build the alternate-choice question. It also goes on your middle finger because, if you give size too much focus or let it be the main focus, it's like sticking your middle finger up all by itself, and that could get you into all kinds of trouble. So don't focus too much on size. Just use it to offer a good alternate-choice close on the size agreement.

Agreement number four is your amenities or your features. The other reason people store at particular storage places is because they like the security and the convenience features. So find the best features of your property that have to do with security and convenience and build some phrasing and questions that will allow you to get agreement on amenities. "Well, what's great about our store is we've got an access-control gate so that only tenants can come and go with their PIN code. And we're well fenced and well lit. So you can tell we take security very seriously here. After all, isn't that what you're looking for in storage? Plus, our storage is really convenient to use because one of the great things we have is a covered unloading dock so that you can pull in out of the sun and out of the rain and unload and load your belongings. What's neater than that?" When the caller says, "That is really neat," you've got an agreement on convenience and security features.

Your features and your amenities are what build value into your offering. Most people think one storage place is pretty much like the next and that all they are renting is dead air to fill up. But that isn't all they are getting. They are getting the peace of mind of knowing their goods are safe and secure. They're paying for the conveniences you offer. They're paying for the security and the perceived security. They're paying for great customer service. They're paying for a lot of things that they wouldn't even know about if you didn't tell them. When prospective renters agree that you have built a good offering with good features and amenities, it's easier for them to justify paying the rent.

Features and amenities go on your ring finger because, if your prospect agrees you have a really good place to store, it is like they have become engaged to being your next customer. An agreement on amenities is like an engagement ring.

Price is the fifth agreement. Price goes on your pinky finger. Prospects have got to agree that your price is reasonable. They don't have to agree that they like the price. Most times, callers have no idea what storage is all about, and they think that price is the most important consideration. Price is not the most important consideration. Everyone wants to know that his or her money is well spent, but convenience and value are the things that people really are concerned about. So until you've had a chance to get some agreement on the convenience of the location and the amenities of security and convenience, callers don't know what your unit is worth. You've got to make sure they know that value. "A ten-by-ten is worth a hundred dollars because you have … (this amenity and that amenity and the other amenity)" So, price is the fifth agreement.

Price goes on your pinky finger because even though you might think it is the most important consideration, it is much less of an issue than the other four.

How do you get through the first four agreements before giving the price? Let's look at the concept of the price stall for a minute. The first words out of that caller's mouth might be, "How much is a ten-by-ten?" You think you need to respond directly to the question. Stop and think about this for a minute. If you give the price right away, then you are enforcing the prospect's notion that price is the main issue. Bad idea. People often lead with the price question because they don't know what else to say or because they erroneously think price should be the main consideration. Here are a couple of things you can say to get the chance to go through a few agreements before you give them a price.

Price stall number one: "Let me pull up my price screen; and while that's loading, let me tell you a little bit about us. Now how soon did you say you were going to need something? Oh, okay, great! And do you know where we're located over on 5th Street? Okay, well then you know we're a really great place to store because we have this convenience and that convenience. Sounds like it's a convenient place to store, doesn't it? And we also have this security feature and that security feature, which means we take security very seriously. And after all, you do too, don't you?"

Wow! Before you know it, you already have three agreements out of the way, and you haven't even talked about size. You still haven't given the price, and the caller is perfectly fine with that because your price screen is pulling up. Now up comes your price screen. You can talk about size, figure out price, and set a time to get the caller in the store. Few people will argue with this price stall because they do not assume you know every price off the top of your head. They understand that it takes a minute to load a computer screen.

Price stall number two: "In order for me to quote the right price, let me just ask you a few questions." That's hard for someone to say no to. They're not going to say, "No, just tell me the wrong price." They're going to let you ask them a few questions, and so you start: "Tell me how soon you're going to need something. Do you know where we're located, and is that a good location for you? Well, this is a great place to store because we have this feature, which means … and that feature, which means …" Now before you've given the price, you've gotten several agreements out of the way.

Price stall number three: "A lot goes into the price of a storage unit. Let me tell you what your money buys you here." Well, now we're starting to build a value proposition right from the beginning. This person is not going to interrupt you because you've already offered a value challenge. The caller will want to hear why your place is worth it. So now you've got a chance to build some agreement before you go to price. Using this price stall means you begin by bragging on your property's features, get some agreement on features and then move into your timeframe and location agreements.

Price stall number four: "Since availability affects pricing, tell me how soon you're going to need a unit, and I'll see what's available." Now you're doing all kinds of things. You're getting permission to get a little more information, you're building urgency right away, and you're letting the caller know that it's not always that easy to get a storage unit. This is a great one to use, too: availability affects pricing.

The easiest price stall is to just ignore the price question and say, "Sure I can help you with that. How soon are you going to need your unit?" Then go right into your qualifying questions. Few people will protest with this approach, and it is easy to master and easy to say.

Okay, let's review these price stalls because you've got to use them verbatim until you really learn them. Don't just try them in your own words to begin with or you'll end up saying something like, "Let me pull on my price, and while I'm loaded, tell me let you something!" You can imagine the kind of reaction you might get to that!

One, say, "Let me pull up my price screen; and while that's loading, let me tell you a little bit about us." Two, say, "In order for me to quote you the right price, let me just ask you a few questions." Three, say, "A lot goes into the price of a storage unit, and let me tell you what you get for your money here." Four, say, "Since availability affects pricing, tell me how soon you're going to need a unit, and I'll see what I have available." Five, say, "Sure I can help you with that. How soon will you need your unit?"

These five strategies are how you allow the caller to allow you to build some agreement, to let you build some value before you give price. Most people have no idea what a storage unit costs. Cost should be the last thing you discuss whenever possible. Whether it costs a dollar or hundred dollars, it costs more than storing in their uncle's attic for free, and that makes it seem expensive to first-time storage customers.

You also have to understand that storage buyers have a language all their own. You have to understand that it is a foreign language. "How much is a ten-by-ten?" when translated into English actually means, "Please tell me why I should store with you." If you understand this, then you will be able to use the price stalls effectively. But you do have to use them like scripting.

The reason they call specific sales phrases "script" is because you must use the phrases verbatim. When you see a theatrical play, the actors use the script as written. There are certainly revisions in rehearsals, and there are rewrites after audiences have reacted or not reacted as the author had intended. But the actors say the lines as they are written because they have been carefully crafted to bring a certain reaction from the audience or to give the audience a certain impression or to cause the audience to think in a certain way.

This is also why it is difficult for some people to tell jokes. If they do not tell the joke just right or do not deliver the punch line exactly as intended, the joke falls flat or bombs altogether.

When you have mastered these phrases and know how to get the right reaction from prospects—cause them to think the right sorts of things and paint the right pictures in their imaginations— then you can put these phrases in your own words to suit your personal style or to suit the person you are talking to.

Improvising sales phrases before you know how to use them is like letting someone go target shooting in the woods with a pistol before they know how to handle the pistol in a controlled environment like a shooting range.

Mishandling sales phraseology may not hurt you physically, but you can easily shoot yourself in the foot figuratively. You can cause real damage if you do not master sales phrases before you try to use them as you see fit. You can chase off a prospect, cause a customer to quit doing business with you, or fool yourself into thinking that sales phrases don't work. Chasing off customers and prospects causes real damage to your revenue and to the reputation of your business, both of which need to exhibit positive growth in order for you to prosper over time.

Now, here's my disclaimer on price stalls: sometimes you have to give the price too early because someone says, "Give me the price on a ten-by-ten," and while you attempt to build some agreement by saying, "Oh, great, tell me how soon you're going to need something," he says, "Just give me the price of a ten-by-ten." Now you have to take a different tack; here's how you handle that one: "That ten-by-ten is only ninety-eight dollars, and here's what ninety-eight dollars buys you at our store. At our store, we have this feature, which means … and this feature, which means …"

Whoa! Before you know it, you're building agreement. You've given the price as the customer demanded, but you haven't given the prospect a chance to say something like, "Well, that's more than I'd like to spend," or "I can save five bucks down the road." You cannot pause between the price and the here's-what-it-buys-you phrase. If you pause, you will lose. The prospect will think you have said all you have to say, and he or she will likely end the conversation. Or the prospect will take over control of the conversation, and you will not be able to regain it. If you don't pause, you will be able to build some agreement at the same time as you've taken price out of the picture. This is not a response for the weak or the inexperienced. You need to do this one with confidence and authority, or it will not work.

If you do not use confidence and authority in your voice while giving the price too early, the prospect will think he or she has you intimidated, and the sales process with this prospect will be difficult to guide and unpredictable in its outcome.

If you have to give price too early—"That ten-by-ten is only ninety-eight dollars, and here's what ninety-eight dollars buys you at our store ..."—you need to focus hard on keeping the rest of the conversation on track and focus on getting agreement on timeframe, location, amenities, and size.

There is more importance in the price stall than just being able to build value before talking about price. At some point during the first two or three qualifying questions, you're going to find out whether this person lies in the easy third—do you remember your Rule of Thirds?—or whether that person is in the impossible third, or whether that person is in the third you're going to have to work for.

Say someone calls you up and says, "How much is a ten-by-ten?" You say, "Since availability affects pricing, let me find out how soon you're going to need it, and I'll see what I have available." In response, the caller says, "Well, I talked to my Uncle Joe. He stores with you. He's going to help me move in on Saturday." You don't need to worry about this one. This is an easy third. Just don't blow this one by talking too much, and you're going to be fine.

Now, you're going to get another caller who says, "How much is one of those storage garage things?" You'll say, "Well, how soon are you going to need something?" The caller will respond, "I won't need it for four years when I will retire." That's going to be a whole different call.

And then you're going to get the callers in the middle who you're going to have to work for. These calls are why you're going to have to get good at dealing with concerns. The biggest concern normally is the "not ready." You've gone through your agreements, you feel like you've gotten somewhere with this caller, and you attempt to put a hold on the unit.

First, how do you attempt to put a hold on the unit? You do that by creating urgency with limited availability. "Well, it sounds like you're going to fit into that ten-by-ten. Does that sound like a good unit to you?" "Yes, it does." "Great. Well, since availability is limited, the best way I could help you today would be to put that unit on hold for you. What's your first name?" And you begin your order-blank close. Before you get very far, the prospect says, "Well, wait a minute; I'm not ready to rent anything yet."

Okay. What does "not ready" mean? Does it mean the caller isn't ready to store or does it mean he's not ready to store with you? Ask a few questions. "Are you moving, or do you just need to get a few things out of the way?" "Have you called a few places yet? What did you find?" Find out what's going on with the caller's situation. At some point, he'll say, "Well, really the issue is this: I don't know when my house is going to close. I haven't even called the real estate agent yet. I don't know what I need." You've found out the real story. Now you can help the prospect realize that it would be best to get the storage unit now and be able to stage the house for quicker sale and start getting organized for the move.

Or the prospect may say, "Well, you know, I talked to XYZ Storage down the street, and they're five dollars cheaper than you." Now you have someplace to go with the conversation because you can explain how the value of your place is worth way more than five dollars, and storing with you is the best way to go.

The other concern that people will bring up when you say, "Since availability is limited, the best way I could help you today would be to go ahead and put a hold on that five-by-five. What's your first name? And your last name? And your phone number?" is often, "Oh, no, I'm still shopping."

What does "still shopping" mean? Sometimes that's just a stall that has nothing to do with shopping, so ask the caller a few questions: "Well, have you called a few other places yet? What did you find?" Find out; if the caller is actually shopping, is she shopping for price? Location? Size? Amenities? Is she shopping for a good customer service experience? Go back to your agreements; see what's going on.

Now if the caller is determined to call some other storage places for units first, try this: "Let me give you a few things to look for." Now you're setting the standard. She's going to compare any other place she calls to your store because you're telling her what she should be looking for. "Let me give you a few things to look for.

You should have a facility that has ..." And then go through your list of amenities because, if other companies don't have those features, the caller shouldn't be storing with them.

Or try, "Have you called a few other places yet?" You'll hear what your prospects have to say. They may say, "Well, we like your price a lot, but we don't like your location," or "We like your location, but we don't like your price." You'll find out what potential customers' concerns are so that you can really understand them.

Another thing you can try is saying, "Well, so that I have a better idea how we might be able to meet your needs, tell me a little more about your priorities." Wow, now you're going to get a whole story from that person. That's a tricky phrase to do. You've got to really digest that one. Let's try it again: "So that I can have a better idea how we might be able to meet your needs, tell me a little more about your priorities." If you can get some good information from people using this phrase, it'll really help you build value and differentiate your store from the next store and help the prospects talk themselves into spending ten dollars extra to store with you, where they'll be a lot happier.

Another concern that you'll often come up against is, "Well, I have to ask my spouse first." This is normally just a bunch of wallow willows because anybody who is storing something has already talked to his or her spouse about it. They're not just calling out of the blue, unless you're dealing with the marriage breakup situation. That's another story entirely, and people in a marriage breakup certainly don't need their spouses' permission to get a storage unit. So a lot of times "I need to talk to my spouse first" is just an attempt to fake you out.

Here are a few ways to find out whether it's true or whether someone is trying to put a move on you and dodge a decision. Ask the prospect, "Well, have the two of you already talked about storing?" Oh! And have you decided what you're going to store? And have you decided when you're going to need to store?" If the caller has already talked about it with his wife, then the risk that he'll get in trouble with her if he reserves a storage unit with you is next to nothing. The risk he's taking is making the phone call and *not* reserving the unit because, if he's already discussed all of this with his wife, he'll not get a good response at home if he hasn't made a reservation or rental. If he goes home and says, "Honey, I called the storage place; it sounded great," his wife is going to say, "Did you get a unit?" If he says, "No," she'll say, "Well, why not? What are you waiting for? Can't I trust you to get anything done?" You can save your prospects from having this conversation if you help them decide to rent now or at least to reserve a unit.

So let's talk realistically about how the partnerships between you and your renters work. If callers have already talked about storing, then the best way you could help them would be to take the hassle out of this situation and reserve a unit for them: "Well, if you've already talked about storing, and you've already pretty much decided what you're storing, wouldn't your wife (husband, partner) be pleased if you went home later and said, 'Honey, I have it all taken care of. That's one less thing we've got to worry about. They'll have the unit ready for us Saturday.'" Now your caller will go home a hero.

This works great most of the time. If somebody says, "I have to ask my wife," "I have to ask my husband," or I have to ask my partner," use the three-question response. It will not work every time. But when it does not work, it is a great setup to invite both partners down to the store to look around and select a unit that they can agree on. Setting an appointment for both spouses to take a quick tour is never a bad secondary outcome of the conversation.

In the worst-case scenario, you can tell the spouse you are talking to all the reasons why the other spouse will like storing with you, so he or she can be your proxy salesperson and close the deal for you. This will work especially well if your proxy salesperson can create a little urgency for you.

Let's take another look at building urgency. We dealt with this a little bit earlier; this is so important because people love to procrastinate when it comes to spending money on things other than the things they love to spend money on. "Limited availability" is the key phrase because the fact is, you never know who's going to rent something from you tomorrow; and particularly in the busier eight months of the season, someone could rent you out of ten-by-tens quickly. So, limited availability is a true condition.

You want people to get in their units now so they can start moving in slowly, and they don't have a big crisis when it comes down to zero hour on moving day. Use your limited availability to help those people get in sooner. Here's what you say: "Since availability is limited, the best way I could help you would be to go ahead and put a hold on that unit for you. Now what was your first name?" Then go to your order-blank close. This simple phrase is how you put a hold on the unit for people.

It is your job to prevent someone from having a storage crisis. If you work at a storage property already, you have certainly had people show up at five minutes to closing time in a moving truck looking like a sweaty, dirty, frustrated mess. And they need a storage unit right away. You have also had people who talked to you last month show up at the store only to find out the unit they wanted is sold out or the special they wanted to take advantage of is finished. Do not let this happen to people. Keep them from having a storage crisis by getting them in their units now.

What I have hopefully given you in this section is a way—a structure, a few specific sets of techniques—to take that call from "Hello" to "When do you need it?" to "Oh, I understand your concern, but here's why our place is a great place to store" to "Let me hold that unit for you; I'll see you Saturday" to "Here's your receipt and thank you for storing with us." This is an intentional process you need to learn, just as you might learn any other process. Work on it, and you will see excellent results.

To Rent or Not to Rent: Getting Inside the Renter's Mind

The question is to rent or not to rent? Many times, we think that our customer is a mysterious animal, and we'd like to get inside his or her head. So I'm going to take you on a little trip inside the mind of our prospects and customers.

This is the question people ask themselves. I'm sure you all realize that most people who need a storage unit are not in a happy time in their life. Even if they're getting a storage unit because they just got their dream job in their dream city, and they're going to be making three times more money than they were, and they will be living by the beach, they still have to move. Have you moved recently? Would you rather cut off a toe than move again? Okay, maybe that is a little extreme. But unless you have professional packers and movers do the entire process while you are on vacation, moving is not a joy.

After we moved the last time, I promised my wife the next time we move, I'm just taking my toothbrush. I'm leaving everything else behind. We'll have the auction people come in, clear out the place, and we'll start over. Now that we've been in the house a few years, I think the next time we move I'm not even taking my toothbrush. The moving process is not a pleasant experience. The process of settling in after a move also takes a lot of energy. It's a crazy time for people.

Let's continue to assume that self-storage is a selling game. This means you are selling to people who are not in the best frame of mind. You know my first rule of selling—you can't sell anyone anything. All you can really do is help people make up their own minds and help people talk themselves into buying from you. In other words, you sell things to people not by selling to them but by helping them sell themselves. Now that's kind of a round-about way of getting to the sale, but how you shorten that is with a technique, a tool, a way of thinking that's called, "assuming the sale."

It's a very simple mind game that you play with yourself. You assume that every person who you talk to is going to rent from you. This isn't just a simple bit of positive thinking. It's a powerful tool: a powerful stance. If you believe every person you talk to is your next renter, then you will treat them like your next renter. Since people act the way they are treated, they will act like your next renter. When you treat them like a renter, they have to talk you out of the rental, rather than you talking them into the rental. If you take that approach with people, you will have the kind of confidence in your property, in your presentation, in yourself that will really become infectious.

When have you dealt with salespeople who were sure you were going to do business with them? It's pretty difficult to say no to the offering, isn't it? It's hard because you know you're talking to the salesperson because you had some kind of an interest and because you would really like to get the issue off of your mind and off of your to-do list. You don't walk up to the greeter at a restaurant and hear the greeter say, "Well, gosh, do you think you might want to eat with us tonight?" Rather, the greeter asks, "How many? Smoking or nonsmoking?" Then he or she takes you to your table. That's the same approach that you should take with your potential renters. It'll give you a tremendous edge. If you go away with nothing else from this read, learn to play a trick on your own mind to assume that everyone's going to rent from you. That change of attitude alone will boost your rentals immediately.

Assuming everyone who presents him or herself as a prospect is your new renter is only the first step. The next step is to get inside your prospects' minds to help them talk themselves into renting with you. The trick to getting inside prospects' minds is learning their internal dialogue. You know this goes on: As you're talking to your prospects, they're talking to themselves. And you're talking to yourself at the same time. You may be thinking, *Gosh, I hope this person rents from me. I've got one ten-by-twenty left; I hope I can rent it today. Geez, I hope the kids got off to school okay.* You've got all kinds of things running through your head when you're talking to people, and the same thing happens to them.

So if you can say to yourself, *I'm going to rent to these people,* you're assuming the sale, and the assumption becomes the power you need to make the sale. At the same time, your job is to influence, or at least understand, your potential customer's internal dialogue.

You're engaging in internal dialogue right now. You're talking to yourself right now while you're reading this. You're thinking, *Gosh, what's this guy doing? I stayed up too late. I hope my 401K increases in value this quarter. Why is Tron going on and on about this?* You've got all sorts of thoughts going on in your head, and I've got stuff going on in my head too. I'm thinking, *Geez, I hope readers enjoy this. I hope nobody falls asleep reading this.* That's just how it is.

Your job is to find a way to help your prospects realize that they are going to rent from you. You already know they're going to rent from you. They don't know it yet, so you're going to have to help them realize that. This is a very powerful twist to helping you rent to more people.

Part of the challenge at the store is that you very rarely see your happy customers. You rarely have someone walk in the office and say, "Hey, you guys are doing a good job today. I'll see you later." How many times has that happened to you? It's a neat thing to have happen. What usually happens is you get the people who come in to complain about whatever their problems are. It's easy to become cynical about our customers; we think they're all whiners, and they're all spoiled, and they can't be made happy because our thinking is completely twisted by the people we talk to—the folks who are having a problem.

The fact of the matter is the flipside. The vast majority of your customers are happy with the convenience and the service you offer. And even though everyone says they hate to be sold to, the fact is that almost everyone enjoys a pleasant sales process. Just help them realize they're going to rent with you and enjoy it.

This is what goes on in your prospects' heads. They suffer from something called the "is its", and you may suffer from this when you're shopping for things, too. "Is it going to be right for me? Is it going to be too expensive? Is it going to last? Is it going to be a hassle if the thing breaks?" You have all of these "is its" going on in your head before you make a buying decision, and your customer has this happen, too.

Typically, the things prospective renters worry about are: Are you going to charge them more than the unit's worth? Is it going to be too expensive? Is it going to be a hassle? Is the place going to be clean? Is it going to be safe?

Customers want to know that, if they're in their unit at night, they're going to walk out of there in one piece. They also want to know whether you're going to be a pain to deal with or not.

Do you think most customer service and most retail salespeople are a pleasure to work with? If you're like most people, you think most sales and customer service people are uninterested, unprofessional, and annoying. Your customers feel the same way. When they walk into your store, they expect that your people are going to be less than friendly, less than helpful, less than happy to be at work, less than concerned about their situation, and a pain in the neck to deal with. They're already coming in the door with a chip on their shoulder.

Do you secret shop your competition on a regular basis in person or by phone? If you don't, you should try it; it's a very enlightening thing to do. If you do shop them, how many of your competitors are staffed with on the ball, friendly, helpful, do-anything-for-you kind of people? If you find a rep like that, you better hire him or her away! Most of your competitors let people who have no telephone skills answer the phone and allow people who have little or no customer service ethic and usually even less sales skills to manage their facilities. Most of your customers, if you're not the first place they've called or the first place they've come to, already expect you to be gruff, unhelpful, and annoyed that you're being interrupted by a rental inquiry.

So this is what you're up against. Prospective renters come in with a chip on their shoulders, and you're going to have to do something to get that chip off. Because they assume self-storage staffers are jerks, they don't want to tell you what their real concerns are. They're afraid that, if they open up to you, you're going to take advantage of them—that you'll rip them off and give them a crappy storage unit for way too much money—or you're going to use the information against them. So rather than tell you their concerns, they're often going to tell you all kinds of other stuff.

You will have people call you up or walk in and say, "I've never stored before. What am I supposed to do?" And those people are easy to talk to because they're open to learning and open to suggestion. But most people don't approach you like that. Most people will say, "How much is one of those?" and try to give you the chip off their shoulder and pass it on to you.

Prospective renters act that way because they're worried. What are they worried about? They act like they're worried about spending too much money because that is a respectable and accepted worry. These are the things they'll tell you to express that worry: "It's too much money." "I have to talk to my spouse." "I'm not ready to do anything." "I have to shop around." "I'm just checking prices."

That's what they tell you, but is that what they're thinking? No. What they're thinking is they'd really rather hit themselves on the thumb with a hammer than have to go find a storage unit. They're now in a situation that's not happy; it's interrupting their day. In fact, their whole life is interrupted, and they've got all kinds of things they'd rather be doing. They don't want to spend any more money than they have to. They don't trust you because most of the retail people and customer service people they typically deal with are rude at best, and they're wishing they had another option. So how do you overcome that?

You have to be the one who overcomes these preconceived notions of you and your storage place. It is up to you and your front-line people because the prospects are judging you the whole time that they're talking to you and you're talking to them. Don't you do this when you're in a restaurant? From the moment a server walks up to you and says, "Hi, I'm so-and-so. I'll be taking care of you tonight," aren't you already keeping score to decide how quick and how responsive he or she is? Is he or she taking care of your water glass? How much are you going to tip him or her—is this going to be a 10-percent tip, a 20-percent tip?

I have a great example. I had lunch one time at a trade show with some folks who I see at a lot of the trade shows, and we had an enjoyable chat about all kinds of stuff, but we had one of those disaster-service lunches. Nothing went right. The kitchen didn't get any of the orders right. It took two tries for Peggy and Jack to get their food right. It took the staff four times to get the right plate out to me. And we weren't the only table they were having trouble with. You could see other tables getting re-served. It was a small disaster in the grand scheme of things. I mean, it wasn't that big of a deal. I got my lunch, and I got to have some good conversation; the food was actually good, so I was happy. But the interesting thing about the whole situation was how flustered our waitress was the whole time. She even sent somebody else to take care of our table because she couldn't handle it anymore.

The folks I was sitting with, Peggy and Jack, said they were at a restaurant a week earlier at home, and it was a disaster, too. It was not only a disaster for getting food on time and getting the order right, but the food was even terrible. But the waiter they had did everything he could to make it right, and they were so pleased with how the waiter handled things and the efforts he made to try to make things right, that he ended up with a good tip.

This is what people are looking for when they deal with you too. They want you to try to make their experience a good one. You don't have to try terribly hard; you just have to try. Prospective renters don't really care if your facility is first-generation, second-generation, A-class, B-class, Or C-class. They don't know the difference; they don't care. They just want to know how you treat them.

As an example, let me ask you this: If your customers—your renters—had to write a check for their rent today, how many of them would know who to make the check out to? When they come and stand at the desk to write a check to you, don't they have to look around to see who to make the check out to? You're probably laughing a little right now; it's true, right? Who do renters store with? They store with the manager. They usually know your manager's first name, right? They don't often even know the name of the company. People want to know who they are dealing with. They want to know that person will try to make things right. If they feel that way, then it doesn't matter what the name of the company is or what promises or advertisements the company makes.

So while they're talking to you, from the moment you say, "Hello," they're saying to themselves, *Is this guy going to be a jerk? Am I going to like this guy? Is he honest? Is he ripping me off?*

You see, people aren't stupid. They take a look at your storage facility, and they do the math in their heads really quickly. They figure your building costs are way less than other kinds of construction. They figure you get killed by real estate taxes. They figure your payroll is next to nothing in comparison to revenue. They quickly count up how many units they think you have and multiply that by the rent you are asking them to pay and say to themselves, *Oh, my gosh! This place breaks even at 43 percent occupancy. Oh, geez! It is a gold mine for the owner, and I'm going to get screwed.* Do you think potential customers are stupid? They know what they're looking at.

So when prospects talk to you and they're concerned about price, they want to know if the person behind your desk thinks it's a good price. If they believe the person behind the desk thinks that you charge too much, you're sunk. That's why your staff has to assume the close; they have to be comfortable with what you charge; they have to believe that your place is a good value for the money. If that's the impression potential customers get, then they'll accept the price for what it is. They accept that your people know what they're talking about, are honest, and have confidence in their offering. What's wrong with that?

However, if your staff expects that every prospect will have sticker shock, and thus, they gives the price hesitantly and then duck for cover so they aren't hurt when the prospect yells, "It costs how much?!" you're sunk. The prospect thinks the squirming that your staff people do is because your staff people think your units are too expensive and a lousy deal. This reinforces any initial impression in your prospect's mind that price is a determining factor in choosing storage. It also makes your staff price-shy and causes them to tell you that the reason rentals are off pace this month is because the units are priced too high.

If, instead, your staff people are calm and confident about pricing and focus on the value your facility offers and the convenience of doing business with you, your prospects will accept the price for what it is and will see the issue as a matter of value and not a matter of price. Everybody wants to do business with somebody who can instill confidence in a purchase like that, don't they?

Feeling confident in a long-term relationship is also important to your prospects. They want to know if you're going to be a jerk if they have a problem; everyone expects there will be a problem with someone they do business with at some point or another. And really, if you have a problem with a company, do you get annoyed about it if they address the problem and take care of you? Rather, you say to yourself, *Whatever. I had a problem; they took care of me. Fine.*

Customers do not mind having a problem with your company as long as there is a reasonable resolution, and the people they deal with in your company are professional about helping them and don't act like jerks.

Prospective renters want to know that, if they have a problem with your company, you're going to be okay to deal with; and they start thinking about that from the moment they start talking to you. That's why prospects will often ask you a lot of questions up front, especially about policy issues and processes. They want to know if you have a customer friendly approach or not. If they perceive your staff person as being great, you win. If they perceive your staff person as being lousy, you lose.

I'm sure you've heard this before, and if you haven't, you need to know it: *a great manager can make a lousy property great, and a lousy manager will make a great property lousy.*

A great manager understands the internal dialogue your customers experience and can address those concerns correctly. If you go out and shop your competitors, you may find a company whose property hasn't been painted for twenty years; yet they're full and only 2 percent off of the highest market rates. You do the math in your head and figure the place is running at 110 percent economic occupancy. You're thinking, *How is this possible?* Then you go in and talk to the manager, and you find out that the people running the place are friendly, knowledgeable, capable, and helpful. You realize, *I'm screwed! They have the right manager.*

Then you go down the street to a newer facility and find a beautiful, well-situated store that's been having trouble breaking 60 percent occupancy for three years; their prices match the old dump that's full that you just visited. You go inside and find out why.

I had this experience at one of the major "player's" stores. I like to do personal shopping because you can pick up a lot of interesting impressions. I walked in to this particular store and said, "I think I need to get a storage unit today." The store manager had her back turned to me and was reading a paperback book. She turned around and said, "You have to call the phone number on the wall there. They can offer you the special; I can't." And she turned back around and went back to her book! I said, "Ah, excuse me. I need to get in today. Can't I just do this with you?" She said, "No, you have to call the number up there. I'm getting ready to go to lunch anyway." And she turned back around again! I said to myself, *Wow! This is great. I wish I had a place across the street from them. This is wonderful.*

Do you think people care about marginal price differences when they can get such a very different customer experience? Do you think they care that much about features, amenities, or updates, when they are really looking for someone who can offer a decent experience?

The problem is, of course, that this "lousy experience" is what people often expect from you. If you understand this and have a good experience waiting for people, they'll become your customers. The experience doesn't have to be great. It just has to be good.

Why do people really decide to rent or not to rent? If you've seen some of the studies, you know that location is still the number one reason why people pick a place to store their stuff. So right away, if a prospect tells you he likes your location, he'll have tolerance for features and for price. He'll have tolerance for all kinds of things if he really likes your location.

Renters like to have perceived security. You don't have to have armed guards in the place; prospects just have to look at your place and say to themselves, *Yeah, it looks like the place is pretty secure.*

You don't have to promise them security. In fact, if you promise them security, the attorneys who specialize in self-storage will knock you over the head. Your customers just need to feel like you've taken enough security precautions so their belongings are likely going to be secure.

The appearance of your place also has to be nice. You don't have to have Renoirs on the wall or professional landscapers come in every other day, but the place has to be comparatively clean and neat. That's what prospective renters expect. Even if they're going to keep their own unit junky, they want at least the rest of the place to look clean and neat. And they want some amenities for their money. They want to get some value for their dollar.

Let me ask you this: do you drive a Kia automobile? Chances are very good that you drive a vehicle more expensive than a Kia. Why don't you drive a Kia? It's effective transportation. It's got a hundred-thousand-mile warranty. It's well designed. Why don't more people drive Kias? Because people want more for their automobile money than just basic transportation. They want something else for their money, so they drive more expensive cars. If you don't have the Kia of storage facilities, it doesn't really matter, does it? People are willing to spend a few extra dollars to get a better location, more perceived security, and a few more amenities. And what they're really willing to spend money on is the good attitude of your staff. If you have a good attitude, people don't care if it costs a few bucks more to store with you. They're happy to do it because they know that, if they have a problem, you'll take care of them.

There are plenty of places to rent tools and equipment in Columbia, Missouri, where I live. If I need to rent a power tool or a garden implement, I go to Lindsey Rentals. Renting tools there is a great experience. It's not a sparkling clean place. It looks kind of like a big tool shed with all the grease and dust you might expect. But it's a fun place to rent. It's fun because the owners and staff know their customers, if not by name, then by face. And when they recognize you, they tell you off-color jokes, give you grief, tease you, and otherwise give you a hard time. As the customer, you are expected to tease them back, give them a hard time, and share a few laughs. It's fun just to stand there and watch the exchanges between the staff and the regular customers, especially the commercial and construction customers. Lindsey's way is a wonderful way to run this type of business. And it seems to be a great way to get your regular customers coming back for more. Can you imagine the potential loss of income if someone who regularly rents a backhoe for six hundred dollars a day goes to rent somewhere else?

I have no idea if Lindsey's prices are higher or lower than anywhere else. I don't care. I assume they are not very much higher than anyone else's, but I may be wrong. What I know is this: spending time and money to do projects around the house may be enjoyable at times. But most projects are not pleasurable; they're a chore. Spending money to rent a piece of equipment is painful. Spending time to go get the equipment is a pain in the neck. Most people who rent equipment are guys. What makes us come back to this tool rental place is the little bit of pleasure we get from poking fun at the owner and getting picked on in return. Sherman and Billy, who own Lindsey Rentals, have, by accident or by design, found a way to balance out all the displeasure and discomfort involved in renting tools and turn the whole experience into a pleasurable one.

I bought a used lawnmower from them recently. I have learned that there are people who leave their mowers for Sherman and Billy to repair and then abandon them. Being the thrifty person that I am, I discovered you could buy a two hundred-dollar mower for sixty dollars this way. This particular mower needed a little work. It seemed to have some dirt in it that was making it stall. I took it home, and it ran fine for a few minutes. Of course I was disappointed. I took it back to Sherman at about half an hour to closing time on Sunday afternoon. Sherman stopped what he was doing and opened up the mower to flush out whatever dirt had been missed the first time. He didn't have to do that, but he did. He could have let it wait until his mower technician came in on Monday. But rather than complaining to you about having to take my mower back a second time for a simple fix, I am telling you what awesome customer service you can get at Lindsey Rentals. A potentially big pain turned into a simple and unexpected pleasure.

We all have our own shopping styles and preferences. No matter how you slice it, shopping and buying comes down to basic pain and pleasure stimuli and response. We are subject to conditioning. Places and actions that we associate with pleasure we seek to experience again. Experiences that cause us pain we seek to avoid. Your customers go through this process during every contact they have with you.

Do a simple experiment. Make two columns on a piece of paper. Title one "Pain" and the other "Pleasure." Then walk through the entire process your customer walks through while dealing with you. Make a tick mark each time you think something causes pleasure and one each time you think pain is the result. You may be surprised at the number of tick marks on the pain side.

How much pleasure or pain does your customer expect? Expectation is the filter through which your customer views and internalizes the pain and pleasure of dealing with you. An expected pain does not hurt as much or last as long as an unexpected one. An expected pleasure does not feel as good or last as long as an unexpected one.

What pains are unavoidable or common to all suppliers of your service? What pains are unique to your operation? What pleasures are common to the shopping experience your customer could have at any of your competitors? What pleasures are unique to your operation? The answers to these questions differentiate you from your competition, for better or worse.

Let's drill it down just a little further. What pleasures offset which pains? Which pains offset which pleasures? If a pain is not offset by some sort of pleasure, then the pain does not go away. In the same vein, a very nice pleasure can be erased by a corresponding pain.

Let's look at a typical storage experience. Joe and Edna are building a new house. There are all sorts of pains and pleasures involved here. Hopefully, the expected pleasure of having a dream home will sustain them through the process. But their existing home sells more quickly than they expect for the asking price. There is pleasure in knowing they got what they wanted for the house and that they will not be carrying two mortgages. However, the new house isn't ready, and they will have to live with Edna's parents until it is—major pain here. Their entire household will have to go into storage. That means they will have to move twice. That means they will be living away from the things they hold dear. Their routines will be interrupted for months. They will have to deal with Edna's parents. Joe and Edna need counseling and a week at a spa more than they need storage. But they stop by your property because Edna passes it on the way to work. This could be pleasure. She is going into a place she is familiar with because she sees it every day. Hopefully your curb appeal is nice and this causes her pleasure.

How does it go from here? Is it a pain or a pleasure to deal with your store staff? Is it pain or pleasure to select a unit, sign the lease, and put a lock on your unit? Are the painful parts of the process offset by some simple pleasures?

You run an audit on empty units and on cash transactions. Why not run an audit on the customer's experience? Mark each transaction, impression, and experience as: 1- expected pain, 2- unexpected pain, 3- expected pleasure, or 4- unexpected pleasure. If a pain is cancelled out by a pleasure, indicate that. If a pleasure is cancelled out by a pain, indicate that.

Now you have a framework from which you can begin to manage the experience your customer has while dealing with you. Roller-coaster operators, toymakers, and restaurant developers have been managing the experiences of their customers forever. Use some of these questions to determine your next course of action. What pains can be avoided? Which pains can be minimized? Which pains can be offset by a corresponding pleasure? Which pleasures can be enhanced? Which pleasures are so fun or so unexpected that they set the tone for the whole experience?

Remember the self-storage operator who has a fresh batch of chocolate chip cookies at the counter at all times? He thinks the cookies allow him lots of room to make mistakes in handling customers because everyone just loves the cookies. Sherman and Billy at Lindsey Rentals don't need to do anything better than their competitors. They can even get away with doing a few things worse. They can get away with causing a few unexpected pains because the pleasure of having a belly laugh when you hear Sherman insult one of his best customers is worth the time and expense of driving to his shop and renting something.

I'm not suggesting you do a your-momma's-so-ugly contest with your customers or that you bank your operation on the toll-house chocolate chip recipe. But you do need to find something fun and pleasant at your store. It may be as simple as having a pleasant retail atmosphere in the office, having the manager step out from behind the desk to greet people, or having a quick check-in process.

If you don't do something to audit and manage your customers' experiences, you leave too much to chance. Run an audit of your customers' experience and see what you find out.

People would rather spend their money where they're treated well, wouldn't they? How many times have you walked out of retail stores because you weren't acknowledged when you were standing around twiddling your thumbs waiting for some help? I've done some informal surveys on this question and find that usually three-quarters of an audience at one of my speaking engagements will raise their hands on this one. Your customers feel the same way.

Price is usually the third or fourth reason for choosing a storage unit. But it's often the first thing out of a prospect's mouth when he or she asks you about storage, isn't it? "How much is it?" does not mean what you think it means. You likely live in an area of the country where many languages are spoken. Even in my home town of Columbia, Missouri, a community of maybe a hundred thousand people, there are something like forty-two languages spoken by children in the public school, which includes an English for nonnative speakers program. Remember that the self-storage prospect speaks a foreign language. "How much is a storage unit?" actually translates into, "Please tell me why I should store with you."

Here's why people don't rent from you: A lot of people talk to you about storage, but their needs change. They reconcile with their spouses; they don't get divorced. The job falls through. Their kid actually does get his own apartment and moves out with his stuff. Their needs change, so they don't really need storage anymore. Sometimes people look into storage while they weigh their options when dealing with a particular issue, project, or circumstance. If you don't help them realize that storage is a great solution for anyone and everyone and for every situation, they will often decide on another course of action. We probably talk 10 to 20 percent of our rental inquiries out of using self-storage.

Money is a factor in why prospects don't choose storage. Some people don't have discretionary income available. Most people are spending more than they bring in as it is. Many people don't know what storage costs. If someone is on a tight budget and fifty dollars is too much for them to spend, then eighty dollars is too much for them to spend. If your competitor is getting eighty dollars for a unit, and you're getting one hundred dollars for a unit, and someone thinks storage costs fifty dollars, you both lose because the prospect won't store with anybody. So if you want to get around people's price sensitivity, you have to find out what they're budgeting for storage, what they think storage is going to cost them, and then work within their limits.

So price will be a reason why people decide, *Do you know what? I'm just going to put the stuff in the dumpster. I'll have a yard sale. I'll give it to Salvation Army.*

Or maybe your facility was dirty the day a prospect visited you. Maybe you got busy and forgot to sweep out the front walkway. Maybe you've been walking by the trash on the curb because you just walk by it every day and you don't bother to look at it. Maybe your attitude was lousy that day. Maybe you had a fight with your kids before you sent them off to school that morning, and you took that bad attitude to work with you. Potential customers are very perceptive. If they think your attitude is off, they don't think, *Gosh, he might be having a bad day*, they think, *What did I do to annoy him? I'm dealing with somebody else*, and they're gone. Right?

Customers don't care why your attitude is off. It's easy to accidentally chase someone off. Here's what happens: you're talking to a current customer at the desk. Someone else walks in. It takes you four seconds to make eye contact with the new person instead of two. That's over his or her tolerance limit; that person is out of there and on to the next storage place. People can think you had a bad attitude even though you were trying to be helpful. People are very quick to judge attitude, so you have to be very aware of that and be prepared to meet or exceed their desire for a good experience.

Here's what happens when you've done well with your customers. Their internal dialogue sounds like this: *Hmm, well, I don't really want to spend a hundred dollars, but I guess if that's what it costs, that's okay. She's pretty nice. It looks like a pretty clean place. I've got other things to do; I can't spend all day on this. I might as well just get this done. Okay, fine.*

If you can help that person's internal dialogue sound like this— *Seems like nice people. Seems like a nice enough place. Seems like the money's not too bad. Okay, I'll do this*—then you're in like Flynn. The next thing they ask you will be, "How do you want me to pay you?"

How many times have you been standing at the counter or showing someone a unit when the prospect turns to you to say, "Well, do you take cash, check, or credit card?" This is a great moment in the sales process. You have helped them talk themselves into renting from you.

Now usually you do have to ask them to rent from you, or you have to say, "Well, here is the paperwork; all I need you to do is fill this out." If the potential renter's internal dialogue is going in your favor and you remember to ask for the rental, you will win … and the customer will have his or her storage needs met. You both win.

I don't know what your statistics are at your properties for lengths of stay. If you don't know, then you need to find out. Guessing an average length of stay is great as a quick thumbnail, but you need to know more than that for making good long-term decisions. You need to know how many people stay a month, how many stay two months, how many stay six months, how many stay twelve months, how many stay twenty-six months, and you need to know those numbers by class of units. You need to know by small, medium, large; you need to know the difference between homeowners, apartment renters, students, and military. You need to know all of these statistics to be able to run your business well. If you don't know your statistics, take some time and start making some notes. If your software that runs your property doesn't give you all of this information, you're going to have to find a roundabout way to get it. There are a lot of facilities where people are staying more than a year at a rate of sixty percent. That is enormous. That means that every effort you put into figuring out how to sell to more people has a serious payout.

Have you ever considered how many businesses have a larger ticket than self-storage? Think about it for a minute. Now ask yourself, what's the average ticket at your place? Six hundred dollars? Eight hundred dollars? A thousand dollars? Whatever it is, who's got a bigger ticket than that? Automobile dealers. Upscale clothing stores and furniture stores maybe. The emergency room, certainly. Apartment communities. Home remodel and roofing and siding contractors. Maybe there are a few businesses that do have a larger average ticket, but how many of them have the kinds of margins a successful storage operator has? I bring this up because, if all you do is walk away from this book thinking it was nice of me to share some of my experience and insight, then you are missing the point. The point is that the effort and expense it will take you to turn your self storage place into a sales and marketing machine will be well worth the investment.

Now, you probably have a whole lot of people who stay just three months, but that's okay, too, isn't it? If they're pumping up your occupancy and you like your rental rates and you're selling them boxes, locks, insurance, and you're renting them a truck, and making sure one out of three of them refers a friend to you, aren't the short termers great for business, too?

I also bring this up in order to point out to you that you have tremendous upside in increasing average lengths of stay. One very real effect of turning your self-storage facility into a sales and marketing machine is the better experience your current renters will have.

You do have to resell your current customers to a certain extent every month, don't you? Are you actively reselling the people who moved in last month? Are you even thinking that way? Well, think about this for a second: What would it do to your bottom line if you could increase your average length of stay by just one month? What would that do to your occupancy levels? What would that do to your discounting strategies? Wouldn't adding an extra month to every one of your tenants have enormous results? Don't your tenants think to themselves every month, *Hmm, should I stay or should I go?* The Clash song would be a great song for customer service, because that's what your tenants are saying to themselves every month. *Should I pay? Should I move out?*

Some of them are thinking, *Should I get a different size unit?* Do you have a strategy in place to upsize or downsize your current tenants rather than letting them move out? If you see people move a bunch of stuff out of their unit, you can ask, "Hey, do you guys need to get into a smaller unit?" If you see somebody cramming more stuff in their unit you can ask, "Hey, do you guys need to get a little bigger space?" That's a pretty powerful customer service touch. Many of your customers think you stopped caring about them when they signed the lease and only pay attention to them if they are late on the rent. The mere fact that you notice them and continue to keep their best interests in mind could easily result in an extra month's rental.

Until your customers see their storage unit as a part of the household, as an extension of the home, they're thinking every month, *Should I stay or should I go?*

Until a business that rents with you sees their storage unit as their back office, as their garage, as their satellite facility, they're thinking the same thing every month: *One more expense I don't really need. Call the storage people up. Cancel the darn thing.*

Now, there are some important thresholds that people will cross over, and you have to be aware of this. The first threshold is the first month—the first time their first full month's rent is due. If you do any kind of specials or discounts, you've moved someone in partly because they got a cheap deal to get their first month. Now their first full month's rent is due, and they groan, "Ugh, time to bite the bullet." And then the second month, "Ugh, here we go again." And then the third month, "Oh, geez, this is getting expensive! Should I stay or should I go?"

If you can get them past the third month, the fourth and the fifth month don't seem quite that bad. And then the sixth month comes, and they go, "Gosh, I've been here about half a year now, haven't I? Do I really want to be there that long? Should I stay or should I go?"

What do people tell you when they move in about how long they are going to need a unit? Do you ask people, "How long are you going to stay with us?" What do they say? Most will say only a month or two, or a few months, right? Yet often half of them are staying over a year, right? Why is that? It's not because they're stupid. It's not because they forget to move out. They're happy. Or at least they are not unhappy enough about the storage unit to do anything about it. It's become their extra attic, their extra garage. They learn to love having it because they can hide stuff in there that they don't have to clean up or deal with or put away.

I heard someone say a wonderful thing at a seminar I was giving. I asked the audience what they thought people were really buying from us when they rent a storage unit. I always get some similar responses when I ask this question: room, space, peace of mind, security for their belongings. Yes these are all a part of the purchase. But here's what someone told me that day—it's a simple and elegant response: What are people buying when they rent from you? They're buying time. They're buying time to decide what to do with their stuff. They're buying time because they don't really want to take care of their situation now. That's especially true if they're moving or they have had a death in the family or they've got some favorite items that they just don't have room for now or they've got four lawnmowers when they really only need two. They're buying time to figure out what to do with their stuff. Isn't that a wonderful way to look at that?

And they're obviously buying a lot of time, if half of them are staying more than a year. Be aware that these thresholds of decision happen, that these are the points when people typically stop and examine what they're doing and decide whether to move forward or not.

So you have to resell your renters each month because each month their resistance lowers. With every time they pay you, their resistance lowers because paying you becomes more and more routine over time. If this is the seventeenth time now that they've seen the automatic deduction on their bank statement or the automatic charge on their credit card, it does not have nearly the impact as the second or fifth time. When it becomes routine, it becomes a part of their monthly experience. When the payment is also associated with feeling good about buying time, the renter stays another month. The storage unit becomes an extension of the person's home and lifestyle.

When you first got a cell phone, did you think "I'm not carrying that stupid thing. I'll leave it in the car, or I'll put it in my purse and keep it turned off"? Do you now carry your cell phone on your belt or in your pocket? Do you now have a cell phone and a PDA? The same thing happens in self-storage. Acceptance, usage, and experience encourage further acceptance and usage over time.

Here's why people stay with you: It's convenient. It's an easy place to hide stuff, get stuff out of the way, keep organized, deal with seasonal items, and keep from cluttering up the house. If you're in a business, it is much cheaper to store your files in your storage facility than it is to take up part of somebody's office. Businesses need to buy time, too. They're always moving people, cubicles, and desks around. It buys them time to deal with their excess inventory and their excess furniture. They don't have to decide what to do with things now; they can stick things in the storage unit; they don't have to worry about how the decision will be made or who has to make it.

Another big reason why renters stay is because it's a bigger pain to move out than it is to pay, and that's the simple equation. People pull out their checkbook and think to themselves, "Nah, it'll be a big pain to move out. I'll just write the check."

Or they look at their credit card statement or their bank statement and see the charge to you. They think to themselves, *I've already spent a bunch of money on storage. But you know what? It would be a huge pain to decide what to do with my stuff and even a bigger pain to move out,* and they stay another month. This is exactly the thought process and behavior you need to stimulate in your customers.

If, on the other hand you have made it a pain for them to stay, they pull out their checkbook and think, *Do you know what? That SOB at the storage place was rude to me the last time I rolled through there. I don't have to take that crap. I'll show him. I'll just move out one night this week and to heck with him.*

If you can't get your billing systems straight, customers will say to themselves, *Those idiots over-locked me again after I paid my bill on time. I'm done with them! I'm moving out.* If you have caused this sort of thinking in your customers, they don't care if it takes them all weekend and they have to miss the football game they have been waiting three months to watch on TV, they'll come pull their stuff right out of there, and you'll be stuck with an empty unit.

A lot of times, renters move out just because the situation that caused them to rent a unit to begin with has worked itself out. The estate has settled. They've figured out what to do with all of Grandma's antiques. The new house finally got built after all of the weather delays. They were finally able to get the contractor to come back and finish. They have everything all settled, so they don't need the storage unit anymore.

Or sometimes renters move out because they're cutting back. They look at that checkbook every month and go, *Hmm, I've got lessons to pay for for the kids, and they need new shoes again. Honey, we've got to get rid of the storage unit.* That happens. However, if you have made their storage experience pleasant enough, renters in this situation will often delay the actual move-out date a month or two.

You don't want a single renter to move out because you had a lousy attitude. You can't let yourself get caught having a bad day; when nothing is working right in the office, your public face can't show that. You have to make sure your customers feel respected and cared about, even if they had what you thought was a silly problem. You can't let on that you thought it was a silly problem. If that's what they picked up from how you handled them, they will think to themselves, *I'll fix you*, and they'll move out.

If your systems stink, you will lose customers needlessly. Is your gate broken more than it is working? Do you have trouble with your access system, so every time renters come in to use their access codes, their code doesn't work? If so the customers will think, *Ugh! Why am I paying for this? I could just leave this stuff in a box in my garage, and it'll be fine.*

Or maybe you've now over-locked a renter three months in a row after he or she has actually paid the bill. One of the top complaints we get from current customers in our call center is from people calling to tell us, "I gave you a check three days ago. Take the damn lock off my unit!"

So, if your systems stink, fix them because it's the easiest way to keep customers.

There are all kinds of ways you can make it easy for people to stay. Some of the most popular ones, which you're probably doing already, include allowing customers to pay via electronic funds withdrawals from their checking account or via automatic charges on their credit cards. Those are easy ways to make it less of a pain for people to pay.

Be sensitive to what's a pain and what's a pleasure at your facility because there's always some kind of balance there between your access, how the doors roll, which way the sun is shining in people's faces, the smell of the place, where dust tends to settle, and all kinds of little things that can make a difference. There are a lot of factors that could create a bit of a pain for your customers. Be aware of that, and either find some way to compensate for each pain or eliminate the painful factors.

It is hard to tell from customer reactions what is causing them pain at your store because your typical customers do not want to confront you. Yes, you have some who come in to the office and say, "Look, this is the second time this has happened. If it happens a third time, I'm moving out. So whatever your problem is, fix it!" Have you had customers like that? Every now and again, perhaps. You've got to love those people because you know if you fix the problem, they'll stay forever. They will feel good that they confronted you, you did what you were supposed to do, and now they're happy. If only all of your customers who were annoyed would do that, your average length of stay would probably double. But that's not what most people do, is it? Have you ever had lousy service at a restaurant and said nothing about it, tipped 15 percent anyway, and just never went back? We have all done that. That's exactly what our customers do too.

If someone says to you, "Gosh, we're moving out. It's been so swell. Thank you." You do not know if they are being sincere or not unless you ask them more questions about their experiences with you. Otherwise, you have no way of knowing if they're driving out of your parking lot, thinking, *That SOB, it's the last time he'll see me!*

You have done that to people, haven't you? Sure you have; we all do that. We say, "Thank you. It's been nice dealing with you," and then we mumble our true feelings under our breath when we have turned our back to walk away.

So be aware that some percentage of people are moving out because something happened that was a pain to them, and you're completely unaware of what that pain was. If you'd only known what this pain was, you would have fixed it.

So if you want to know how your customers are answering the question, "Should I rent or should I not rent?" you have to listen to your customers. If they're giving you feedback, you have to ask them a few more questions. And you've got to anticipate the concerns that people are going to have because most people have the same concerns I have been writing about for the last several sections.

The concerns that new renters have should be posted on the screen in your mind's eye. Don't you get many of the same questions all day long? Yes, sometimes you get some interesting, off-the-wall inquiries, but it's usually the same questions. You know what people's concerns are; so do things to anticipate those concerns and show people that you have "it" covered. We know what people are looking for. We know what bothers people. We know what they're trying to avoid. We know what they're afraid of. We know what they like in storage. Let your customers know that you know all these things, and they will feel much better about choosing you.

If your customers are not talking to you, then you have to talk to them. You have to find some ways to get them into the office or get them on the phone or by email because most people are pretty busy. They don't really want to stop and visit with you. They have twenty-seven things on their to-do list, and they still have to-do items left from yesterday to get done. They really don't want to stop and visit with you. So get them in the door! Send them a coupon for 10 percent off of boxes, put fresh-baked cookies on the counter, wander around the property when people are out there accessing their units and visit with them. Find out what their concerns are. You may not know half of what their concerns are because you're busy doing what you need to do to run the property. And it is difficult to make the time to visit with customers because there is always some fire for you to put out. You have to make the time to go out and talk to people and find out what they're thinking about. The very fact that you bothered to ask some renters will get you another month's stay out of them. Find out what they're really concerned about because many times people won't tell you their real concern until you've talked to them for a little while.

Do you coach and counsel your employees on a regular basis? What's the response you get when you say, "Hey, how's everything going?" Your employee says, "Fine."

If you don't ask a second question, you won't have a single clue what's going on in his or her mind. The same thing happens with your customers. When you say, "Hey, how's everything going?" and they say "Fine," you have not gotten any information. You have to ask specific questions. Then you find out that the unit that they're in gets flooded with debris every time they have the door open and the wind blows, and it's annoying the heck out of them or whatever their real concerns are.

If you do at least a few of these things you've read about, fewer people are going to choose not to rent. Fewer people are going to choose to move out. Here's the one thing you should also consider: what is the cost of doing all of this? There is no cost, because everything I have written about comes down to your attitudes and perceptions. Those are all free. Anything you do from this book will improve your business and improve your revenues. It will take a little bit of self-examination. You have to catch yourself when you're having a bad attitude. You have to catch yourself when you're not up to par in your customer service and do something about it. So there is some cost to your pride and your self-esteem from time to time.

But what's the potential impact on your bottom line? It's huge. If you increased the conversion rates of the number of people you rent to compared to the number of people you talk to by even five points, what would that do to your business? What would it do to you if you increased your average length of stay by only one month?

You'd be looking at expanding your facility because your occupancy would be so high and your rental rates would be at the top of the market.

You have four jobs in front of you if you want to implement the strategies and tactics I have laid out for you.

1. Create a selling culture

2. Learn the basics of sales

3. Apply sales skills to self-storage

4. Get inside your customer's mind

Each one of these activities will bring you big rewards in building a better business and in pushing profit to your bottom line. I wish you good luck and good selling!

Tron Jordheim's Bio

Tron Jordheim is one of those entrepreneurs who is always making something out of nothing. He started his first business in the sixth grade with a roll of paper towels and a can of window cleaner. He has been at it ever since. He took his interest in protection dog training and created a whole new business model that put him through college. Tron was one of the people who helped New York City start its police canine unit. He ran man–dog security patrols for Pan Am airlines at JFK airport and was the team captain for the United States team that competed at The European Championship for German Shepherd Dog Clubs in 1982. He was sought after as a seminar leader and training advisor for competition dog clubs across the country.

When the flip-flop in international exchange rates took the profit out of his business of importing German Shepherd dogs from Germany and Austria, Tron went to work as a cold-call salesperson for the Great Bear Bottled Water Company in New York City. Great Bear gave him the Upper West Side of Manhattan, which was the worst performing territory in New York. It wasn't long before it was one of the best performing territories, and Tron was being sent out to work in other markets as a trainer and salesblitz leader. Great Bear was eventually taken over by the Perrier Group and its Poland Spring Water division, which made known its intent to eliminate the sales force and fire all the Great Bear middle management people.

That's when Tron decided to move to central Missouri, where the commute is short and the prairie wind is bitter. Once in Missouri, Tron saw that a Culligan Bottled Water franchise was trying to make a business grow and went to work to help make that happen. Tron helped grow the business from one thousand two hundred customers to six thousand eight hundred. It became the Culligan Bottled Water franchise with the highest per capita penetration of bottled water accounts of any in the nine hundred plus dealers in the Culligan network.

It wasn't long before Tron became a verb; after training and consulting for other bottled water companies and other Culligan dealers, salespeople stopped going selling and started going "Troning" to get more customers. His booklet, *Setting Coolers*, and his work in the field are two of the reasons many of you use water five gallons at a time.

After Coke and Pepsi decided to get into the bottled water business in a big way, Tron decided to look for other opportunities. As it turned out, the massive distribution network of Coke and Pepsi and the convenience of small bottles of water did cause the five-gallon water business to plateau dramatically. And then along came an opportunity to grow the PhoneSmart business from the drawing board. Tron not only grew the roll-over sales support end of the business but also launched a successful secret shopping/quality assurance business unit and an Internet lead distribution unit.

Tron continues to be sought after as a public speaker, sales trainer, and consultant. His success as a speaker and trainer was affirmed when he was recently accepted as a member of the National Speakers Association. The National Speakers Association is the premier group for public speakers in the United States. There are strict criteria one must meet before being accepted, which puts Tron in with the cream of the public speaking crop. Look for Tron at national and local self-storage events. His sessions on sales, marketing, people management, and business development are worth the travel.

CPSIA information can be obtained at www.ICGtesting.com
Printed in the USA
LVOW091435111211

258854LV00002B/189/P